BE A MAN

BE A MAN

HOW MACHO CULTURE DAMAGES US AND HOW TO ESCAPE IT

CHRIS HEMMINGS

Biteback Publishing

First published in Great Britain in 2017 by
Biteback Publishing Ltd
Westminster Tower
3 Albert Embankment
London SE1 7SP
Copyright © Chris Hemmings 2017

ISBN 978-1-78590-167-6

10 9 8 7 6 5 4 3 2 1

A CIP catalogue record for this book is available from the British Library.

Set in Minion Pro

Printed and bound in Great Britain by
CPI Group (UK) Ltd, Croydon CR0 4YY

This book is dedicated to the legacy of my dad, who taught me and my brothers to be strong. And to my mum, who taught us all that it wasn't necessary.

A special mention must go to Zoe, too, for being my reluctant yet patient echo chamber.

CONTENTS

INTRODUCTION

Turning thirty doesn't scare me anymore.

It sure as hell used to. By the time you reach thirty you are clearly a man – right?

Well, I'm only a few months away from it now, and I'm left wondering what the transition from boyhood to manhood should have looked like. I don't feel like a man. I never really have. I don't feel like a woman either, before you start to think that's where I'm heading. Nor do I feel or act how society dictates I'm supposed to at thirty years old. Wife? Nope. House? Yeah, right. Well-paid job? Well, I'm a journalist, so...

So, where have I gone wrong? Or have I? Young boys are often told to 'grow up' or to 'be a man', but why should they? What are the rules? Who makes them? And who says they should be followed?

Using some of my own experiences and those of many other fascinating people, I'm going to look at the reasons why we should stop brainwashing kids, teenagers and adults with archaic notions about what a man can, and should, be, and do what I can to redefine what masculinity means to all of us.

My hypothesis is simple: traditional masculinity is still seen by far too many as something desirable, despite it causing huge problems not just for those in its pursuit, but for society as a whole.

You may be asking why you should pay attention to a not-yet-thirty-year-old man about all of this. 'He clearly hasn't lived enough life to have valid opinions on all of this', I hear you say. But don't worry, that's just your inner-man putting up his defences – we've all been there.

The reason I hope you will listen to me is because I've experienced the pursuit of masculinity from both sides of the fence. I've attempted to be the big, strong alpha lad and I've also given that up forever – and have since found my life to be infinitely more rewarding.

I'm sure you'd like some proof, so here it is. In mid-2006 I found myself in a room of forty blokes all of whom, at the time, I considered to be my friends. I was coming towards the end of my year as a university fresher, and these men were all members of the rugby club.

As is the tradition, orders were barked at 'freshers' and must be obeyed. Resistance to play by these rules once or twice means a severe forfeit or punishment. Outright refusal means being unable to socialise with your teammates. On this occasion the order was clear: 'You're on door duty, Hulk [short for Hulk Hogan, my nickname within the club]. If any birds try and get in here, you have to slosh them.'

For the uninitiated, the verb 'to slosh' means to throw a full pint – preferably of something colourful like snakebite (a mix of beer, cider and blackcurrant cordial) – directly at someone's face.

So, there I was: snakebite in hand, poised for action, ready to carry out the unquestionable will of a group of men who would suffer no consequences for my actions. Suddenly, I see movement: a pair of female legs at the top of the stairs, slowly descending towards me. At first, I didn't care too much. I'd done this numerous times before, each time receiving the adulation from my club-mates I felt I fully deserved. Only, this time was different. This time, my friend Holly was looking for her friend's birthday party in the student union. She was dressed up as one does for a party and was, unfortunately, about to enter the wrong room.

The fact that she was a friend changed everything. 'Sloshing' a random person meant little risk of remorse, whereas doing it to a friend would have repercussions. I turned to the group and, not then understanding the gross double standards of my words, protested about having to pour my drink over someone I knew. To no avail, however. The orders were clear, the deed must be done. So, reluctantly, I mouthed 'sorry' and covered her in purple booze.

She was understandably furious. She looked up to see forty shirtless men chanting, laughing and high-fiving at her expense; and, before her seething fury turned into full blown rage, she was powerless to react and quickly left the room, holding back her tears.

Out of sheer embarrassment I didn't speak to Holly again until half-way through our second year. I'd actively avoid her on nights out and around campus. Then, at the end of the Christmas term, I sucked it up and sheepishly offered her a lift back home to Manchester. It was during that journey she told me how I'd made her feel that night, explaining not only that I'd ruined her clothes and her evening, but also how degrading it was to be mocked by a room full of lads after essentially being attacked.

You may be wondering why I'm painting myself in such an awful light when I'm trying to convince you to read my book. The thing is, I believe it's that dreadful place I've come from that has allowed me to have a first-hand understanding of how so-called masculinity damages not only the young men caught up in it, but everyone else around them.

In order to explain this in more detail, I'll have to tell you a bit more about myself.

CHAPTER ONE

BE A MAN

From as early in my life as I can remember, I struggled with what was expected of me as a boy who would one day become a man.

I come from a fairly traditional family unit of Mum, Dad and three sons – of which I am the youngest. Both sets of grandparents comprised a stay-at-home mother and working father. My parents were no different. My mum had, until her second-born arrived, worked. But on the day he was born, she decided to give it up and look after us full-time.

As the third of three boys, I was always suspicious of my parents' motives for having me. Aside from my brothers' constant teasing, my parents readily admitted that they had been trying for a girl. Katie-Jane would've been my name… or Brother Number Two's had he been born without a Y chromosome.

Sport played a huge role in the day-to-day life of the Hemmings family, and it quickly began to define who I was as a

1

person. I became incredibly competitive both on and off the sports field, spurred on by constant competition between me and my siblings. My dad drilled into us the importance of toughness, both mental and physical, as a means to achieve both our sporting ambitions and those beyond the pitch. For him, toughness was key. Crying was for girls, and he had no problem telling us that.

I vividly remember the day he dropped me off at my swimming lesson and the teacher told me that I'd been promoted to the next group. As an eight-year-old boy, with nobody around to reassure me, I cried. I cried and refused to swim. When my dad came to collect me from the pool and was told that I'd 'got upset', his face quickly turned to an expression of sheer embarrassment. That his son would cry over something so minor was simply unacceptable.

I learned my lesson that day: boys don't cry, and I fought back my tears as much as possible from then on – albeit often unsuccessfully.

My dad wasn't the biggest or toughest man in the world, but he certainly exuded strength in numerous other ways. He was a selfless man and would always do anything in his power to make other people happy. I can't recall ever seeing him in a moment of emotional weakness. This remained true until the very end; his unwavering positivity was apparent even as he lay dying, knowing full-well he was drawing his last breaths.

The way he approached his illness and protected us all from its harsh realities is something I will never forget, but don't let me paint him as some gruff alpha male. The more I reflect on our lives with him, the more I realise he was trying to be anything but that. He was merely a product of his upbringing. His father, my grandfather, was a man for whom flashing a smile was a possible display of weakness. He was stoic in the face of adversity, stoic in the face of triumph – hell, he was even stoic in the face of gardening, pretty much the only thing he admitted to enjoying.

In that respect, my dad changed his stripes. There was something of the modern man about him, and it must've been one heck of a battle for him to make it as far as he did. He may have been out being the breadwinner, but he used to relieve my mum of parenting duties the moment he stepped foot back in the house. Not because he felt any obligation but, as my mum now tells me, because being a 'hands-on' dad was the most obvious thing in the world to him. It hadn't been the treatment he'd received from his father. He clearly wanted better for his own kids and to give them more in return for the love they gave him.

From as far back as I can remember, he told me he loved me. He hugged me, kissed me and, as such, both Mum and Dad were the one to go to with a grazed knee – though my mum actually had more of a stomach for the truly gruesome stuff. In later life, Dad had fewer issues with talking through his feelings with his children or laughing at himself, although there was still a strict filter in there somewhere and his emotional release would only ever go so far. He never did quite make it all the way in that respect, but he gave it a damn good go.

He was what I like to call a 'transition man', stuck between the rock that was his own father's emotional ineptitude, and the hard place of his desire to be better. I don't have children yet, but I look at how my two brothers have taken to fatherhood and see that our dad's desire to be a brilliant father is an example they've both taken to heart.

There is an innocuous memory from my childhood that has always stuck with me. I was sixteen and out for a walk with my mum and dad and I had my arms wrapped around and inside my giant then-fashionable woollen cardigan to protect myself from the bitter Pennine wind. 'That's how girls walk', Dad said, tapping my arms so they fell by my side. My mum, leaping to my defence, shouted, 'SO WHAT? He can walk how he bloody well likes.'

That tiny moment summed up my early misgivings about the pursuit of masculinity. I'd seen girls walk like that and thought it an excellent solution. I'd seen men next to them, arms out wide, striding into the chill and wondered why they bothered.

The need to be warm over the desire to look manly is a microcosm of something I grappled with for the next few years and, unfortunately for me, I let the wrong mentality win.

As I matured through my mid-teens, for reasons unbeknown to me at the time, I began to try and fit in with the images of masculinity I saw all around me. At an all-boys school it became paramount for those, like me, out on the sports fields to be the champions not only of our sport, but also of our gender. We were meant to be the role models, the towering juggernauts of masculinity striding around the school with an inflated sense of pride.

I'd been on the football team for the first three years of high school, but puberty was harsh on me and I soon became too fat for the football pitch. So, in the winter, despite being utterly useless and not even liking the sport, I took up rugby.

I vividly remember being told by my dad, my brothers and some teachers at school that I wasn't cut out for rugby. I was 'too soft', they all said, making a less-than-subtle dig at my lack of masculinity. Despite never having had a desire to play the game before, and rather than accept I was soft and choosing to play something else, I set out to prove them all wrong. Rugby was a big test, and it was through playing rugby that I developed my ability to fake my toughness, my strength and my manliness. I managed it for years, with the belief that being a part of the rugby team made me a bigger, better man.

Even at school, being a rugby player gave you an inflated sense of self-worth. First XV ties were given to anyone who played for the team regularly, and were worn as badges of honour to distinguish you from the lesser mortals who weren't sportsmen. There had been unpleasant behaviour exhibited by the boys in the football club, as the 'banter' and 'lash' that go hand-in-hand with competitive sport were a regular feature, but it was through being a rugby player that I began developing some seriously negative character traits.

This carried on all the way through to university, where I once again joined the rugby club. I'd actually tried to hide on trial day (perhaps recognising an inner desire not to continue down that road) but was dragged out of bed by some friends. I soon found myself a part of a group of men loathed by almost everybody on campus.

During my first week I'd not only had my head shaved like a monk, with my hair Sellotaped onto my top lip (hence the nickname 'Hulk Hogan'), I'd also been forced to strip naked and run through the canteen in my student halls after being made to down litres of cider as punishment for disobeying the demands of the older members. Mostly, it seemed, university rugby socialising was about being naked against your will. It was a simple way for the senior club members to find out who their rivals were in the 'big penis' stakes. It was willy-waving on an industrial scale.

If you wanted to earn your place within this oh-so-great club as a fresher, you had to leave your morals at the door. Despite some of these men being the same age as you, they took their dominance extremely seriously and acted with utter impunity towards those, like me, who were at their disposal. We were bullied and humiliated, all the while being told to harass people who weren't in the club. Some of it may have counted as what's described as 'harmless banter', but it was insidious and our actions were increasingly abhorrent.

There was one game that became very popular during my first year called 'Hot Leg'. The rules were simple. Find a girl in a club, get her to dance with you, then, when she's grinding on your legs, you piss on hers. The aim of the game was to piss as long as possible until she noticed. Then, once she did, to try and hold on to her for as long possible, still pissing.

This was just one of a whole host of disgusting activities that marked our behaviour as something far beyond anything that could be described as light-hearted. It was the ritual humiliation of women, something that was ever-present in the way we acted day in, day out. It was always about proving something to the group; your ability to drink more than the others, to have more sex or to be more outrageous. If you think masculinity has nothing to do with it, let's look at the time I was in the pub with some female friends and was forced by one of the club members to put myself on display. I was told it wasn't acceptable for me to be 'hanging out with birds' and was not only coerced to drop my trousers and stand next to some of the well-endowed seniors who had found me, but I was also made to drink pint after pint until they were satisfied I was too drunk to socialise with my friends.

I can truthfully say that I didn't participate in some of the worst activities (Hot Leg being one of them), but I certainly was involved with many of the awful things we did. I didn't have the guts to question what was taking place or to say no, as the fear of social rejection or punishment was too great.

That is my biggest shame. My frame of mind was trained solely on proving my masculinity to such an extent that I couldn't disassociate myself from the group and didn't allow myself to empathise with those we were affecting. To say no would have been social suicide, so I obliged my teammates' whims. I took the constant name-calling and embarrassment on the chin for an entire twelve months, all the while carrying out the orders of my seniors. It was exhausting.

Within the club, masculinity was king. There was a constant battle for supremacy in everything we did, with no concept of caring for anyone we hurt – even each other. On tour I fell ill with acute tonsillitis, a condition I'd regularly suffered from, only to be made to drink washing-up liquid for 'being wet' and refusing to participate in the end-of-tour 'lash'.

It was a perfect example of how disgracefully men can treat each other when there is no mutual concern for well-being. How these men treated their teammates was bad enough, but how they treated others was truly appalling. It reflects a more universal truth about men and the ways we stifle each other's emotional development – something that is a major focus of this book.

I got so deeply mired in the whole masculine charade that I was even elected to be the club's social secretary in my second year. I'd tried so hard to be manly that I managed to convince fifty of the blokiest blokes around to put me in charge of their booze-fuelled rampages both on campus and beyond. The activities I organised and the people I was choosing to spend my time with were, mostly, awful.

As a fresher, being ordered around meant I felt a certain detachment from whatever heinous act I was expected to carry out. Be it drinking a dangerous amount of alcohol against my will, sexually harassing women in night clubs or generally being racist, homophobic, misogynistic and utterly obnoxious, I always wrongly felt a lack of responsibility.

Within the first week of second year I'd taken aim at a

fresher who'd clearly lost a huge amount of weight and had excess skin around his midriff. Once all members of the new intake were inevitably told to get naked I became the bully, mocking his loose-hanging skin and pointing it out for all to see. But seeing the distress I was causing him switched something in my brain, and I slowly began to extricate myself from the fresher-baiting.

It was only then I first began to question why we were all acting like this. For the next few months I carried on with being social secretary, but I didn't fulfil the position of dominant-second-year as I was supposed to.

Already questioning myself and my future with the club, I took a trip back home to see my friends and family. One evening I came across the Manchester University rugby team on their social and caught a disarming glimpse of how the rest of the world viewed me when I was out at university. These men were parading themselves around the pub, disrupting other people's evenings and acting with that sense of impunity and entitlement that lad culture advocates. It was that, plus the conversation with Holly just weeks later, which convinced me I was being an utter twat and had to change.

After some fairly simple soul-searching and a realisation that I hated everything about the way I was, I quit rugby for good. From that moment onwards I was in a constant battle to try and stop enacting the masculinity I'd bought into for so long, and over the next few years I began to detangle myself from the restrictive shackles of manliness.

Despite never being truly comfortable with how I was

behaving, I'd been convinced that the macho mentality was the only option available. I now realise that the way I acted was a reflection of those around me and their projections of masculinity.

I often wonder how many of them were faking it just like I was. In later conversations many have expressed similar remorse about the way we behaved as students.

● ● ●

It's hardly surprising that, of all the friends I still have from my university days, zero of them are female. That's something I've changed over the years. I have female friends from before my days of being a lad and I have made numerous female friends over recent years. Listening to them has been a great help in understanding the effect behaviours like the ones I exhibited can have.

While inflicting misery on others is reason enough to give up any sense of machismo, what I hadn't reckoned for was that I might have actually been damaging myself at the same time. The personality I'd developed was one of a permanently sunny disposition. I scoffed at the idea of depression, assuming that people with mental health issues simply needed to 'cheer up'. My emotions were largely ignored, and it wasn't until I couldn't ignore them any longer that I once and for all ridded myself of my profoundly destructive macho mentality.

It came in the wake of my father's death and from a place

of almost infinite sadness. I'll never forget the phone call with my dad when he told me he'd been given three months to live. His cancer had returned, and with a vengeance. He remained calm and composed throughout his final months, a state of being he maintained until the very end. In front of his three sons, he steadfastly refused to show either the mental or physical pain he was clearly suffering.

Knowing that your dad is facing his own mortality puts a son in a strange place. You want to ask questions, but that's increasingly difficult the longer they are batted away by someone so determined to mask his emotions. In the end there was nothing left unsaid between us, but there were questions I wish I'd asked. In particular, I never truly asked how he was feeling. He didn't want to discuss his anguish, just like he never wanted to discuss funeral arrangements. He didn't want to accept that his death was fast-approaching.

So, in the weeks preceding his death, I copied his approach. I maintained a cheerful facade and felt it was my duty to ensure everybody's spirits remained high. Even at my mum's sixtieth birthday party, just days before his death, I acted the clown in front of the family to ensure reality didn't bite. Dad had already told us off over the suggestion the party should be cancelled, and he spent the whole day smiling, surrounded by his family.

But it wasn't long afterwards that reality did take hold and he was rushed to hospital, having lost the use of one side of his body. We later discovered that the cancer had spread to his brain, and that this was it. With the little energy he had left as he was slowly losing function in his body, he still found the strength to hug my mum, to make us laugh and to tap me on the head and tell me off as I sobbed in his lap. Even at that moment, he was teaching me the importance of remaining strong in the face of adversity. Even then, he hated to see me cry. I know he was doing it to protect himself as it must have been too awful for him to know he was dying and hear his son cry, but that moment stuck in my head for months to come.

They say a person's hearing is the last thing to go and, after having lost all motor function, he lay motionless in a hospice bed for almost two days. But I continued talking to him, telling him what was going on, reading him the football results, acting as if he were still alive. Having waited around for him to breathe his last for hour after hour, my brothers and I decided to leave briefly to get some food. 'We're going for a curry, Dad', we told him. 'Nice and spicy, just how you like it.'

Fifteen minutes later my mum called. She told us to hurry back as his breathing had slowed. He'd gone before we arrived. To this day, I'm convinced he'd willed himself to stay alive long enough that we'd have to leave. He chose the moment of his death, knowing that his sons weren't in the room when he finally succumbed to his illness so we wouldn't see him in that final moment of weakness. To my dad, being a man meant exuding strength in all its many forms. His final act was to make sure we never saw him give up.

• • •

After his death I desperately tried to maintain an air of positivity. At his funeral I only allowed myself to cry the first time I put his coffin on my shoulders. I had five minutes alone, cried my eyes out, and then returned with a stoic look on my face, assuming it was what was expected of me and, more importantly, what would have made my dad proud.

As both my elder brothers sobbed through their eulogies, I took pride in the fact I smiled through mine. I don't know why, but I felt like I had proved something. What, and to whom, I still have no idea. I barely allowed myself to cry at all, and stupidly even went back in to work the day after his death. Instead of acknowledging my grief, I found myself ignoring it during the day at work, and escaping it at night with alcohol. Lots of alcohol.

For nearly four months I drank away my sorrows and became increasingly erratic in my behaviour. I was out in Manchester almost every night looking for anyone I knew who was willing to drink with me. My work suffered greatly, and even culminated in one of the senior BBC bosses sending me home for working too many hours and too ineffectively.

The reality of what had happened fully hit me months later in a late-night phone call to my brother. I hadn't slept for a couple of days. I'd decided to give up the booze for a while in order to clear my head on the recommendation of two friends who'd separately told me I had to stop drinking. I actually owe it to them, and my wider friendship group, that I managed to get my life back in order so quickly.

It's only when the rum-filled clouds dispersed from my brain that I recognised my own grief. I suddenly realised that I'd been maintaining a calm front, but beneath the surface I was a frantically sad 26-year-old man. My brothers both had wives to confide in, but my girlfriend had left me shortly before Dad died, so I was alone with my thoughts. Matt and I spoke for at least an hour about how Dad wouldn't see me get married, meet my children or tell me off for looking 'like a scruff' ever again – some of the things I wish I'd spoken to him about before he died.

My inability to process my emotions came from years of learning how to hide them, and it took a great deal of effort to unlearn it all. Once the floodgates opened, I could barely stop talking. From that moment, I spoke about my dad as often as I could. I often worried I was boring my friends, but they always said no, even though I'm sure they were just being kind. Not only were they all incredibly patient, some of them even shared their experiences of loss, allowing me to recognise and understand my own thoughts and behaviours better. In all honesty, without my amazing friends I wouldn't have got through my grief so successfully.

What I soon came to realise is that, as a boy and to this day, I always wanted to cry, share and seek companionship, despite the overriding pressure to always be strong, to be brave and to 'be a man'. The liberation I have since found has enabled me to share my thoughts with many incredible people I've met along the way. And now, if you'll let me, I'd like to share my thoughts with you about men in the early twenty-first century, and how we're stifling ourselves, each other and, most importantly of all, society as a whole.

• • •

But don't let me paint myself as some sort of born-again saint. I'm far from it. Those years spent chasing the masculine dream clearly had a lasting effect on me. Just recently, I became reacquainted with a university friend. We bumped into each other on a night out and had a wonderful time surrounded by mutual friends.

Only a month or so later, she sent me a message to complain about my actions. She said I'd sexually objectified her in front of my friends and I had made her feel extremely uncomfortable. Given that I've been trying to better myself in that department for years, I felt affronted by this suggestion and did everything I could to try and prove her wrong. I even dug out a photograph of the evening with the two of us smiling in it. But I was wrong; she hadn't meant that night. We had, apparently, bumped in to each other at a party two weeks after our first reunion, and I had acted like a complete dickhead. Being too drunk to remember doesn't in any way excuse what I did. She told me, rightly, to 'fuck right off' and said she didn't want to speak to me ever again.

That day I learned another valuable lesson about masculinity. Even as I tried to break free from the extreme version of machismo I had striven for in my early twenties, as a thirty-year-old man, my immature pride meant I refused to listen to someone to whom I had acted terribly. My defences went up, and I accused her at best of misremembering, and at worst of total fabrication.

By using more examples from my own life, I want to demonstrate to you the many ways in which the traditional tropes of masculinity are not only damaging to the individuals directly caught up in them, but also to the young boys who pick up on these destructive patterns of behaviour. What's more, I want to show you how actions in that respect can also have hugely negative consequences for women and girls.

It's taken me nearly nine years of questioning the development of my own masculinity to realise that, while I have to shoulder responsibility for the awful things I did, there were insidious pressures coercing me to act that way. And it wasn't just me and it wasn't just my rugby club. I now recognise how widespread these attitudes are and how easy it is for men to get swept up in the collective pursuit of masculinity. We still see it far too often.

I've already produced numerous radio shows and have written articles about some of the issues I will cover, but it was only when writing this book that I came to see that I had always skirted around the subject and had only a basic understanding of why these problems arise in men. I want this book to help continue some excellent conversations already being had in this area, and believe that it's through honest reflection that we will one day put a stop to these negative cycles of behaviour. I hope to show that by highlighting what many of us believe it means to 'be a man', we can identify the stereotypes among men that have been with us for generations and rid ourselves of the more damaging masculine characteristics.

To find out what these traits are, I spent eight months speaking to school children in Manchester, fathers from Islington and teachers, professors, city workers and a whole host of other male and female voices from around the world I happened to meet along the way.

And so this book is way more than an account of my experiences. It's the combined testimonies of some fascinating people who have their own unique insight into how masculinity has impacted their world, be it on a personal or a professional level.

Those who contributed didn't have to give up their valuable time to help me, so I can only assume they each recognised the importance of highlighting the issues associated within the pursuit of masculinity, whatever they may be.

I just hope we can all convince you, too.

CHAPTER TWO

OUR OWN WORST ENEMIES

At this point, I feel it necessary to address the #NotAllMen brigade who will, I have no doubt, already have their knives sharpened, ready to dissect every opinion shared in these pages. To them, I say this:

So nice of you to engage with this debate. Now, before you start shouting at me for tarring the entire male population with the same brush, I urge you to consider who your indignation should be turned on: me, or those who point-blank deny there is anything wrong? Sure, not all men are violent, but most violent people are male. Not all men are rapists, but most rapists are male. Every man doesn't kill himself, but most of the people killing themselves are male. Do you see a pattern?

Of course, not everything that I say is relevant to us all, I totally get that; but to dismiss the conversation out-of-hand is only serving to prove my point – that traditional masculinity can be as damaging to others as it is to ourselves, and that it is masculinity itself that prevents us reflecting on those very issues. So, for the purposes of this book, I will be using 'men' and 'man' as an all-encompassing term. Instead of getting angry at me for demonising 'all men', why not turn that same passion into something positive? Maybe use it to talk to the less enlightened lads out there? The ones that need a hand on their shoulder and a quiet word in their ear. Let's stop being our own worst enemies.

● ● ●

Martin Seager is a clinical psychologist who's been trying to improve the outlook of mental health in men for years, and he told me about what he describes as the 'masculinity script'. He says masculinity presents itself in three forms:

1. Being a fighter and a winner. It's always been this way for men across our evolution and we learned it in order to protect our families and protect the safety of the species.
2. Being a provider and a protector. Whether hunting animals or going to work in an office, men are trying to earn to provide for their family.
3. Retaining mastery of control of everything possible in their world.

It's hard to argue with any of these descriptions and it makes sense that, as an evolutionary force, masculinity developed to ensure the survival of our offspring. Times were tough for early humans, and the physicality of some men would have been of great service to a tribe roaming the wilderness. But it's been more than 70,000 years since our cognitive revolution. That's 70,000 years wherein we humans have been able to use our brains to better understand the world around us. It's this genetic development that's credited with us being able to cooperate flexibly in large numbers and, over time, we have created not only spectacular real worlds, but also thousands of imagined ones, too. But, in almost all of those worlds, men have put themselves in charge.

Men's natural physical strength is one of the main reasons why, in almost all the societies we've created, men have reigned supreme. In a time when physicality was imperative for survival, it's not surprising that men determined hierarchies and placed themselves at the top. Men maintained that dominance through violence (or at least the threat of violence) and by creating systems that kept them firmly in charge.

It's only been in the last 100 or so years that half of humanity has dared to question men's rights to dominate the sphere of influence. Since the early suffragettes of the late nineteenth century to the most recent fourth wave of feminism, men's perceived sense of entitlement to power has been rightly challenged; and I can't help but think it's masculinity that's to blame for preventing us men from embracing these changes. It's the same men who subscribe to the belief that we're biologically programmed to 'retain mastery' of the world around us who are the most resistant to relinquish the male-dominant status quo.

In a desperate attempt to shift the focus of the issue, a lot of men will blame feminism for many of their problems; but can you really blame women for wanting their half of the pie? They've had the crumbs off our plates for so long, isn't it only fair that they fight back? For years we've tried to undermine the movement in numerous ways, but the women have, rightly, had enough. Now, campaigns such as Everyday Sexism, the Women's Equality Party and even a parliamentary Minister for Women and Equalities all strive for the practical application of gender equality, and ensure that men don't get away with discrimination and sexism, both casual and more extreme. There are now a record number of women in employment in the UK. Women are outperforming men at school and university and are, slowly but surely, earning their rightful place as decision-makers in almost every industry. Progress may not be as fast as it could be, but it's happening.

It's impossible for us to roll back the tide of equality, no matter how much some members of society long for 'the good old days'. The world is changing, and the twenty-first century is fast becoming a place where traditional masculinity is not only outdated, but also undesirable and responsible for many of the ills within our society. And as this happens, men are seemingly being caught in the headlights. We're not quite sure what to do. As a result of more women working and being successful, men are now actually allowed, nay expected, to be involved in their children's lives. But, despite legislation allowing us to, we're hardly jumping at this opportunity; indeed, there's only been a 4 per cent uptake in the government's new shared parental leave scheme.

Well, why should we have to give up our high-paying job while the wife, who earns less anyway, can stick to what she knows best and sort the kids out? And sure, we can take our couple of weeks of paternity leave, no problem, but John Johnson CEO will expect us back at our desks at once. He didn't take any time off when his kids were born, so ten working days must be plenty of time for his employee to properly bond with his child.

I'm aware that I'm stereotyping massively, but what I'm trying to outline is that men are simply not allowing themselves or other men to change their traditional roles – something that desperately needs to happen if we're to stem the tide of male-centric problems.

We have to accept that masculinity causes problems. I know that's an incredibly difficult thing for any of us to ever admit, but it's true. Sure, some of us are lucky enough to be well-balanced and emotionally developed individuals, but there are much wider issues that need to be addressed – amidst which our perceived sense of masculinity is at the core.

In order to dismiss the fact men create problems within the world you need to have been indoctrinated, much like I was, to not see the blindingly obvious. My actions at university were disgraceful, but pale into insignificance when you look at the horror men can inflict not only on others, but on themselves. The most obvious example of this is violence.

When you think about the classic image of masculinity, you'll probably think of big, burly men. That notion has been foisted upon us from a very early age, thanks to the toys designed for boys (more of which later) and the pictures on our TV screens. Men are seen to be tough and strong, so it follows that we become determined to try and prove ourselves to be the toughest and the strongest. And the most simplistic way to do it is through violence.

The comparison between the sexes when it comes to violence is astounding. When you learn that 90 per cent of murderers are male and that only one in every ten violent crimes is carried out by women, it's hard to argue this isn't a male problem. And while male-on-female violence levels are shameful – with two women murdered by their partner every week in the UK – the vast majority of violent assaults are male-on-male.

Men are also far more likely to commit sexual assault or rape, too. When it comes to sexual assault, while most of the victims are female, thousands of men suffer the horror of sexual assault every year – but again, this is a mostly a male-on-male phenomenon.

Masculinity is constructed in such a way that far too many of us resort to violence as a means of trying to control our piece of the world. Many of the men in our prisons today are there because they resorted to either physical or sexual violence, and it's high-time we talked about why it is happening with such frequency.

But we're not just attacking other people. For those of you

who already know this, the following statistic will not shock you. For those who don't, it may just shake you to your core. In the UK in 2017, the biggest killer of men under the age of forty-five is suicide. Just think about that.

Despite all the horrible diseases that exist in this world and all the possible ways we could be dying or killing each other, by the time we reach middle age more of us take our own life than die in any other way. It's a horrific statistic, and one that is echoed in many other civilised societies across the world.

There has been a recent surge in coverage of male mental health problems, but there is still a certain stigma attached to the issue that's dissuading men in particular from talking openly about personal problems. Those with a diagnosable condition are less likely to be in therapy and more likely to self-medicate through alcohol and drugs, rather than open up to friends or family. But men don't just kill themselves because of diagnosable mental health conditions. The NHS website confirms that suicide is 'also linked to worthless-ness and hopelessness'. Feeling worthless or hopeless is far more difficult to diagnose than depression, and is probably something we all feel at some point in our lives; but, for too many men, their reluctance to discuss their feelings means it's becoming deadly.

These statistics tell us that men are in the midst of a crisis. We're depressed, feel worthless and, most importantly of all, don't feel able to talk about it. For those who end up as an unfortunate statistic, something has happened in their lives to make them no longer want to be men anymore. I believe that by identifying the toxicity of masculinity, it's possible to not only reduce the number of young, male suicides, but also see an improvement with regard to many other problems caused by the pressures exerted by masculinity.

• • •

In order to better understand men, let's take a brief snapshot of the male world in 2017. It's undeniable that men still hold the highest positions in almost all influential professions.

There are more male MPs currently sitting in the House of Commons than there have been female MPs in the history of British politics. Only a third of our current Members of Parliament don't have a penis. It seems we're still doing alright when it comes to making the big decisions away from politics, too. If you're a man, you're still statistically fourteen times more likely to be a CEO of a Financial Times Stock Exchange 100 Index company than if you're female. And it's not just good news for the boys at the top. Despite the Equal Pay Act now being 45-years-old, pay discrepancies between male and female salaries range from anything between 13 and 24 per cent depending on whose statistics you believe. Either way, it's clear that the injustice is still rife.

Over the course of our working lives, the average man is likely to earn about £300,000 more than a female colleague, and we're also still far less likely to do our fair share of child-rearing. Many men still see child-rearing as a mostly female occupation, and that helps explain why there are comparatively so few men in teaching, caring roles and other low-paid child-centric professions – something I will discuss more thoroughly later.

Our Y chromosome somehow grants us access to the most visible positions on TV, the radio and journalism. Who wants to listen to a woman, anyway? They only want to talk about the latest overweight celeb, being a mum and that god-awful concept of feminism.

Of course, I'm being an arsehole, and only idiots think that way, but the belief that only men are fit for these roles is deeply entrenched in many male minds. And yet, despite occupying so many positions of power and prestige, many men are still suffering from an existential crisis – so why is that?

The major problem is that our learned sense of being male is almost entirely based on a hideously outdated template that is completely unsuited to 21st-century living. There are a still few core ideals we're all meant to strive for, and there isn't much wiggle-room amidst these visions of idealised manhood when it comes to paving the way for genuine or sustained happiness.

First and foremost, for almost all men, it's about appearing successful. While success can be an extremely broad church, for many men it isn't at all. Too often our success is based on a limited range of pursuits, with a common thread of dominance.

Most obviously, successful men must be rich – or so the story goes. For centuries wealth has been the barometer of male success, and this still rings true with a huge number of us. Put simply, money means we are able to provide for a family – and society tells us that having a wife and children is still the very pinnacle of our existence. We can buy our castles and populate them with princesses and heirs. Once achieved, we really have nothing to worry about. Job done.

Failing that, the least we can do is be the breadwinner. We may not be able to afford an actual castle, but an Englishman's home is his castle, no matter what size. As long as he has four walls and a steady income from a bit of hard graft, a man's job, once again, is done, and his credentials as a man to other men and women are proved.

Men can also prove their dominance by simply being 'hard'. Big, tough, strong men have been considered to be dominant throughout the entirety of Western human history. The Vikings sent their burliest lads to maraud their way through Northern Europe, and the Romans revered gladiators who slayed each other in the amphitheatre. These men were admired by their citizens and feared by their conquerors. Nowadays we have a somewhat watered-down version of this, with men competing for 'gains', muscle-mass and the apparent ability to win a fight. And if we don't have the wealth, stability or strength, we can at least be sexually dominant over women and our love rivals.

So, the apogee of masculinity is, apparently, someone who drives a fast car, wears expensive suits, has attractive partners and pays more attention to their abs than they do to said-partner. These aspirations place an inordinate amount of pressure on men and, in an increasingly difficult economic climate, are becoming more and more difficult to achieve.

The Instagram generation are almost powerless (aside from deleting the app, that is) to stop the onslaught of perfectionism they see every single day. Many of the problems traditionally associated with young girls are now more often being recognised in men, too. For example, a growing number of people diagnosed with an eating disorder are now male, but the true figures may be masked by the fact men are too embarrassed to seek treatment for a 'girly' illness. And yet, despite the pressures of social media, it is actually the younger generations who are pioneering the much-needed change in this destructive masculine narrative.

A YouGov survey carried out in May 2016 outlined the change of heart in young men perfectly. Men of all ages were asked to rank themselves on a scale of 0–6 of manliness, with zero being 'totally masculine' and six being 'totally feminine'. Only 2 per cent of 18–24-year-olds (what the media likes to call 'millennials') say they felt 100 per cent masculine. That's a tiny proportion. In contrast, the older the participants the more masculine they scored themselves. For the 25–49s, 21 per cent answered 'totally masculine'. That jumps up again to 32 per cent for the 50–64-year-old men and up to a whopping 56 per cent when the 65 and overs were asked.

On the surface, this is really good news. It shows that younger generations are liberating themselves from the gendered binary and that they no longer feel simply masculine or feminine. But what it also highlights is that it's the older generation who, both implicitly and explicitly, are putting pressure on their younger counterparts to maintain the masculine ideals that they had been brought up with. So, too many fathers, bosses and high-ranking media personalities still prohibit the progression of a more inclusive environment for those less macho men trailing in their manly wake. This age divide is very telling, and points to the incredibly significant role younger generations have to play in redesigning our world.

For these forward-thinking members of younger generations, equality is almost a given. We (what? I'm still young!) can't imagine there is any other way for the world to work and have grown up understanding equal opportunity is gospel. Those, generally of older generations, who still trumpet meritocracy as more important than gender equality, have a lot to learn. Maybe they'd be absolutely right about meritocracy, if it weren't for some blindingly obvious truths: one, it simply isn't working; two, women have been kept down by a patriarchal society for too long and progress isn't happening fast enough; and three, why shouldn't women be afforded the same privileges us men, one way or another, have all benefited from?

Equality is not a zero-sum game. When women fought for the vote, they didn't do so at the expense of men. When women seek lawful protection from domestic violence, they don't want men to be at greater risk of it. And when women want to be treated fairly in the workplace, of course the aim is for fewer men to rise to the top of their profession, but that is equality in action. One group doesn't gain rights at the expense of the other, but many men are struggling to recognise that fact. Women are entitled to the same power, opportunity and, most importantly, respect as we are. That masculine objective of running the world is stifling us all, because women deserve their equal share, and men need to give themselves a break from the pressure masculinity can exert on them.

While many men see this surge in taking matters of gender equality seriously as a threat to their own manhood, encouraging society to appreciate and utilise the willing female workforce is beneficial to both sexes. Men can't – and shouldn't – do it all. It is neither representative of society, nor good for our mental health. While we might, in typically male stubborn fashion, refuse to acknowledge the change and we might think that we like things as they are, think back to the eye-opening fact that suicide is the biggest killer of men under the age of forty-five. It is no coincidence that the more trapped and pressured men feel to live up to some archaic and idealised notion of masculinity, the more likely they are to end up as a horrifying statistic.

It's time we started asking ourselves some serious questions. What's really causing us to be so unhappy? What's stopping us from seeking help? What makes so many of us turn to violence – even upon ourselves? How can we ensure future generations don't suffer the same fate? And how can we all adapt to fit in with an increasingly equal society?

I hope to convince you that, from the very moment we're

born and in every aspect of our lives, we need to work to upend the outmoded notions of masculinity for the good of us all, and replace these with a commitment to raising more tolerant, kinder and emotionally equipped young men. We have to come together to help release ourselves from the burden that is the pursuit of masculinity.

CHAPTER THREE

BOYHOOD & GENDER

Ask anybody who's pregnant what question they get asked most often. It isn't generally to ask if the baby is healthy, and while we may sometimes ask how far along someone is, the thing we're far more interested in is the sex: 'Is it a boy or a girl?' To be fair, the sex is the first biological fact we can establish about a child-to-be, other than the fact that it exists. But that doesn't go the whole way to explain why it is still the first thing we all want to know.

Historically, a baby boy signalled the birth of a much sought-after heir to a man's fortune. For centuries, it was deemed totally inconceivable for a female to inherit land, wealth or titles. Heads of families have nearly always been male. The men have made the rules, and passed on those powers to other, younger men. Even the Royal Family kept their ancient tradition of male precedence over his elder, female siblings when it came to throne-ascension until 2013 (that it took so long is absurd, but that it changed at last should be celebrated) and a survey taken in 2011 saw that only 60 per cent of major landowners were prepared to allow their daughters to inherit their estates. It took six wives and the death of his son before Henry VIII's daughter became queen, so it's little surprise that baby boys have always been the favourites. Having a healthy boy assured a family's status and finances. It was an assurance of a strong, stable figure to oversee the next generation and that, in turn, placed boys on a higher social pedestal than girls. Boys were primary; girls secondary, and sadly, the bitter taste of those attitudes still lingers to this day.

Before the days of ultra-sounds and eagle-eyed doctors desperately searching for a tiny penis in among the amniotic melee, knowledge of a baby's sex just wasn't available to expectant parents. All they knew was that a second heart was beating and, in a few months, a baby would be born. But as it so often does, technology gives us a head start. That bit of kit now allows us to pigeonhole our offspring before they're even born, and my how we take advantage.

It starts from the very moment we find out. Before we know anything about the individual character of our little boy, we make preparations for turning him into a default man. Bedrooms are decorated in blue with cute but specific animals: lions, giraffes, dinosaurs, with some football wallpaper hanging near the crib for good measure, just next to the fire truck he can play with one day. There's not a butterfly, flower or sparkle in sight because that's 'girly' and we just can't have boys liking 'girly' things.

Once we know the sex, we often use different words to talk to and describe the movement of the foetus. A boy's kick might be strong, while a girl's movements are gentle and delicate. The language we use to speak with and about our children the moment the sex is known plays a vital role in shaping who they will grow up to become. The things we say to young boys and girls train them to learn about their place in the world.

Telling a boy he's done something 'like a girl', where 'girl' has been used pejoratively, reinforces the notion that there are prescriptive modes of behaviour for boys and girls – and that boys are expected to do things better than girls. It also implies that there is a distinction between how boys and girls behave, so young male minds will quickly learn that they can, and should, do things differently to girls: and this is where problems quickly arise.

The title of this book comes from a phrase I heard so many times as a child. It's one of those throwaway lines my dad used to use when he thought I wasn't living up to his expectations. While it might sound like a fairly innocuous admonishment, the use of certain language can have long-lasting effects. Phrases like that are often banded around when fathers in particular are trying to teach young boys the strict lessons of manhood. We tell boys to 'man up', to 'toughen up' and that 'boys don't cry' with frightening regularity, and yet we don't quite understand the effect these words can have.

What we're actually doing every time we utter one of these phrases is telling youngsters that the only acceptable way for a male to be is the classic masculine ideal, which, as we already know, is potentially damaging. We're deriding men for being human. We're telling boys that any display of fear or sadness is unacceptable and must be bottled up. And we wonder why suicide rates in men are so high.

Tony Porter founded the group A Call To Men, which is aimed not only at preventing violence against women and girls, but also at promoting a 'healthy and respectful manhood'. He regularly describes the 'man box' we prescribe to young boys, telling them they must fit in to it if they are to be accepted as a man.

In a now-famous Ted Talk on the issue of male emotions, he recalled the ways in which he raised his son and daughter differently. He says he allowed his young daughter to cry no matter what the reason, and accepted that because she was female. As for his son, crying simply wasn't acceptable. He said 'an alarm would go off' whenever his son cried, and he'd say things like, 'Why are you crying? Hold your head up. Look at me. Explain to me what's wrong. Tell me what's wrong. I can't understand you. Why are you crying?'

Tony was brought up in a troubled home in the Bronx of New York, and admits that toughness and strength were the paramount teachings he got from his father, who even congratulated him for not crying at the funeral of his brother. So he naturally passed those lessons on to his son, and felt the 'responsibility of building him up as a man to fit into these guidelines and these structures that are defining this man box'.

Just like my experience at the swimming pool, far too many young boys are taught from an extremely early age that emotions are somehow feminine, should be stored away and never faced up to. Yet humans are privileged as being the only animals who cry emotional tears. Scientists theorise that it's a trait we developed that helps with the complexities of our moods, since tears contain a stress hormone – so crying literally washes stress out of our bodies. It can be the ultimate release and by promoting a male 'no tear zone', we're depriving ourselves of an evolutionary gift. Science wants us to cry, outdated masculinity does not. There's no evidence to suggest men want to cry less than women; it's merely that by the time we reach adulthood we've been indoctrinated to believe that our tears are a sign of weakness or vulnerability – neither of which are remotely acceptable according to the masculine construct.

In his book *Man Up: Surviving Modern Masculinity*, Jack Urwin examined many of the issues facing modern men while reflecting on his own experiences of depression. He told me he attributes his reluctance to show any emotion from an early age to the onset of his mental health problems, admitting that: 'I'd struggle to cry at all these days. It's gone past the social fear of crying in public. I'm now totally unable to do so after a lifetime of repressing the urge to cry.' He says his unwillingness to show emotion means he 'no longer has the tools to deal with his problems because it was so hard-wired into me that you shouldn't cry'.

The anti-crying rhetoric plays into a larger narrative about male emotions in general. Being told to 'man up' doesn't just prevent us from displaying our sorrow and fear – it instructs us that very few emotions are acceptable to be put on show. Real men, we are told, are allowed three default states. Of course we're allowed to be happy, as that's how we let the world know we're okay; but most of all we are required to coast around in an almost permanent state of apathy.

Men are also allowed to be angry. Masculinity promotes anger as a method that enables us to alleviate ourselves of emotional baggage. Except anger isn't a healthy tool for emotional release and, what's more, it's dangerous. Anger is a precursor of violence, and we already know that young men are far more likely than young women to become violent.

Rather than championing emotional intelligence, we only train our boys in emotional repression. As we teach young boys to ignore their negative emotions, we unwittingly numb their positives ones, too. We start restricting men's ability to experience the full-range of human feeling and offer no support system for sad, fearful or frightened men. This helps to explain why we're so reluctant to seek help when we grow up and start struggling with all the difficulties life can throw at us.

• • •

It's not only language that determines how our young boys turn out. Some believe that boys are genetically programmed differently to girls – and, to a certain extent, I agree.

Scientists are still in disagreement over whether or not the essential differences between the sexes are innate or learned. Leading the research in the blue corner is the Cambridge Professor of Developmental Psychopathology, Simon Baron-Cohen. His work focuses heavily on 'the essential difference' between the brain structures of men and women, hypothesising that the male propensity towards certain societal roles and behaviours is due to men being hard-wired for more systemising tasks, while women are naturally more empathetic.

In the red corner is Cordelia Fine, an eminent psychologist whose work also focuses on neuroscience and trying to understand the ways in which our brains function. Two of her books, *Delusions of Gender* and *Testosterone Rex* examine where the behavioural differences between men and women arise, and she believes it's too simplistic to solely blame our biology. Indeed, it's these lazy stereotypes about male and female propensities that make it possible to dismiss bad behaviour as 'boys will be boys'.

While I'm not qualified to start making accurate analyses about whether so-called 'male' behaviour is something inherent or learned, I want to point out that simply excusing bad behaviour as 'natural' is to do complete disservice to the impact our upbringing can have on who we become. A child's sex is biological, whereas its gender is something learned. In the nature vs nurture fight, I can't help but believe that nurture is our master.

The environment within which we place children has an

immeasurable impact on their identities. After the birth, and save for a sex organ inspection, it's almost impossible for anyone other than the parents to know if a baby is male or female. All babies look almost identical. But to save ourselves and our friends from the embarrassment of three-day-old Oliver being called 'she', we tie ludicrous ribbons around our bald baby girls' heads and we stick our boys in a Manchester United onesie, just to be on the safe side.

Numerous studies have suggested that gender is the first category children recognise. They know before they're able to speak that there's a difference between boys and girls. But where has that come from? Boys and girls don't look all that different from each other at two. Not physically, anyway. So how has it happened that a two-year-old knows Child A is boy and Child B is girl? Humans of all ages have an innate desire to assign everything to clearly identifiable groups. As children get older, they pick up the signposts we've created to differentiate boys from girls.

It happens in every walk of life. Anita Cleare, a child developmental expert, agrees. She told me that 'children's brains are innately programmed to look for categories' and that for the first five to seven years of their life, a child's biggest project is developing the ability to organise and categorise things in their brains. According to Anita, children 'see gender in everything around them, and therefore it's one of the biggest categories they put things in'. And she's right; everything is gendered, and that's particularly true when it comes to products marketed at children.

On a recent visit to my brother's house I encountered just that phenomenon. When I picked up my pink-rimmed sunglasses as I got ready to leave, my five-year-old nephew William came to my rescue. He shouted that 'Uncle Chris is trying to steal Sophia's glasses.' Despite my protestations, he was adamant that pink glasses are for girls only, and so they must belong to his female cousin. I tried to use it as an example of how far society still has to go to catch up.

I've noticed a pattern that emerges whenever the topic of gendered toys and activities is discussed in the media. Two very distinct camps form on both sides of the debate. One (mostly women) talk candidly yet convincingly about how it is time to ditch the labels, and the other (mostly men) shout and protest about how we're trying to feminise young boys. In fact, these attitudes appear when anything to do with changing traditional views of gender is debated.

Here's an example of the trolling I received in the comments sections under an article I wrote for *The Independent* to congratulate Toys 'R' Us for removing gender labels from their toys. It's from a lovely lad who's named himself 'Brutus':

> The obsession with 'gender stereotyping' is a stupid feminist meme. Boys are naturally drawn towards construction toys and warrior toys and girls to dolls.
>
> Neo-progressives are fixated with the idea of re-engineering society to fit their absurd notion of what people should be like.

> There is only one thing I despise more than feminism, Mr
> Hemmings, and that is manginas.

Quite what tucking my penis between my legs has to do with the argument is beyond me, but what Brutus does manage is to neatly highlight a common misconception when it comes to arguments that children are 'naturally drawn' to certain toys. He also admits to despising feminism, but I'll save that for a later chapter.

There've been a whole host of studies claiming to prove Brutus and his ilk's theorem that the desire to play with tools is exclusively reserved for young boys. A US study in 2011 undertaken by Vanessa LoBue and Judy DeLoache sought to demonstrate the extent to which young children's choices are governed by colour. They introduced children aged seven months to five years to blue and pink objects and concluded that boys develop a pronounced aversion to pink before they're even three.

So, the argument goes that young boys and girls should play with toys designed specifically for their gender. 'So what?', I hear you say. By the age of three most children are able to identify whether they are male or female, and I have no issue with that. What's worrying is that toddlers are also able to point out an activity, behaviour or toy they think is suitable only for boys or reserved just for girls. The thing is, and what people like Brutus fail to recognise, is that by making blue trains and pink dolls' houses, we are telling children that they are expected to play with certain toys and not with others. We are teaching children that vehicles and engines are for boys, and clothes and makeup are for girls. Unfortunately, these stereotypes are confirmed as children get older – and we wonder why women make up just 8 per cent of engineers in the UK.

You might still think that toy categorisation isn't a big deal, but the more I think about my own childhood, the more I start to understand how much of an impact toys and games have when it comes to where we fit in to the world.

I remember adverts as a kid for creepily lifelike dolls. The little girls in the adverts cradled them to sleep, fed and changed them, and there was never a little boy in sight – just as there weren't any girls seen in adverts involving army men, weapons and cars. By three years old, Anita says our children have already been brainwashed by gender stereotyping and 'quickly become fixated on what's a girl thing and what's a boy thing'. This male/female binary is something they have learned from us, and, as a result, the sexes start to quickly move apart from one another.

Olivia Dickinson is from the charity Let Toys Be Toys and is doing excellent work trying to remove gender labels from children's toys. She told me that more and more young girls are being encouraged to pick up traditionally masculine toys. She says girls are more readily opting for sports and construction sets, whereas boys are still reluctant to be seen with prams and dolls. While this might seem insignificant, think about the huge advancements in organisations pro- moting female participation in sports such as football and rugby, and yet there's still a greater stigma attached to boys taking ballet lessons.

Despite the progress made by women, however, men remain the so-called superheroes. Olivia pointed to the distinct lack of children's shows or films aimed at both sexes with a female protagonist. Very few items of merchandise for the TV show Paw Patrol feature the one female character, Sky. Similarly, while Rey was the first ever female lead of *Star Wars*, she was, again, excluded from the merchandise. Images of tough men saving the world are streamed relentlessly at children and promote a universal ideal of uber-masculinity. Those calling the shots clearly don't think strong female role models are marketable to anyone, particularly not to boys. Of course, exclusively male and female merchandise exists for the shows aimed at boys and girls respectively, but it seems far more acceptable for girls to play with male merchandise than it is for boys to play with toys featuring princesses and pop stars. Children learn that it's okay for girls to aspire towards masculine role models but never for boys towards feminine ones, which is strange – as I'll explain in the next chapter – since boys are surrounded by women for the majority of their young lives. These male superheroes imply that men alone occupy truly aspirational roles, and this both puts a cap on female ambition and creates anxiety for boys who feel they never live up to these heroic figures of their childhood.

Another example of something apparently innocuous that, in fact, breeds insidious archetypes for boys and girls, is the beloved saviour of parenthood, Disney. Now I love Disney, and a hex on any of you who dare to say the classic Disney movies aren't some of the greatest screenplays ever made. But if you look back over the archives of Disney films there is a common theme. In fact, it's the most classic story you can tell. A beautiful damsel princess, most often in distress, lovelorn and/or locked away by a domineering male character, has to be rescued from her misery by love's true kiss in order that they can have their happily ever after. And who might that noble task fall to? Why, who else, but a strong, handsome prince?

The same goes for Marvel comics, too. The protagonists are 99 per cent male and always 100 per cent awesome. These men are celebrated because they're super strong, tough and show no fear in face of unimaginable danger. And with these guys, it's not good enough for them to save just one girl; they're responsible for saving the entire world! The thing is, being a handsome prince or having super powers is simply never going to happen. Yet despite the impossibility of these goals, we still dress our little boys up as Batman and use a lexicon of strength and bravery when describing their achievements. This remains largely unchallenged and programmes young boys to see themselves as perennially inadequate and the opposite sex as lesser beings.

Toy and game companies will say they are simply meeting the demands of their market, but it is a market that they've created. As with many of these issues, the problem is cyclical. Creating two distinct marketplaces sends the clear message to both parents and children that boys and girls are to be treated differently from day one; and so, the apparent demand for gender-specific toys continues. These companies fail to acknowledge that, by creating separate markets for boys and girls, they are ruthlessly underpinning the gender differences our children learn to recognise in each other from far too young an age.

CHAPTER FOUR

DADDY DAY-CARE

The games I played at primary school are perfect examples of how society influences our subconscious minds. At playtime, there were really only two games that girls and boys would play together. While there were no specific rules, the roles were clearly defined. When playing 'house', the boys would wait for the girls to make them a hearty breakfast of plastic fried eggs and imaginary tea. Once breakfast was over, the men would embark on their daily duties. We opened our Fisher Price tool box, hit things with rubber hammers and used battery-powered drills before inviting the women in to our newly built beanbag forts. As the men built the imaginary world, the women were left behind to chat among themselves before we noble lads allowed them in to our not-so-impenetrable fortresses.

These stereotypes are hard to shrug off. And when you extrapolate these innocent games into the wider world, you quickly see a pattern emerging in terms of what are perceived to be gender-specific jobs. Put bluntly, boys don't learn to value nurturing or caring roles. They are considered 'feminine' and to be avoided at all costs. The effects of this are reaching epidemic levels – just take a look at the shockingly low number of men involved professionally with young children.

Children pick up a very specific skill set from toys and activities. It's widely accepted that traditionally male toys and games encourage, among other things, motor skills and spatial awareness. Meanwhile, young girls are encouraged to play with toys that enhance their social and language skills. Young girls therefore develop a much keener ability to communicate than boys. While this may not seem particularly consequential, let's again recall how men's inability to talk about their problems is one of the major factors contributing to male suicides.

One of the other big factors that lie behind male mental health problems is that men aren't taught to nurture either themselves or each other. In short, they don't learn the importance of creating a caring and open environment. Think of all the activities you'd traditionally associate with girls. Take, for example, playing house or hopscotch and skipping. There's a clear theme that runs throughout all of these activities, and that is cooperation. But there's another thing they have in common, too; they don't involve any hint of competition. Each of the girls involved will work together in small groups to achieve overall enjoyment. There is usually no hierarchy, and no attempt to create one. Girls' play reinforces the importance of cooperation, protecting friendships and seeking solutions where all participants are successful, instead of establishing winners and losers.

While boys are also encouraged to engage in cooperative activities, such as ball sports and video games, these pastimes also have a very competitive edge. Boys learn how to compete, be aggressive, take risks and mask emotions in order to be successful. By occupying their assigned role in the hierarchy, both on their own team and against opposition, boys learn how to become leaders and also how to win or lose without becoming emotionally involved with their competitors. Whether or not you believe that female brains are more naturally wired to empathise, it's clear that the activities we push young boys into don't encourage its development.

A child's mind is so malleable that it can be taught almost anything. Unfortunately, what boys and girls are learning is that empathy is reserved for girls alone. This is something I discussed with Michael Flood, an Associate Professor of Sociology at Queensland University, who focuses on shifting certain cultures among men. He told me that a lack of empathy is a huge determining factor when it comes to violence prediction among men. He says, 'we make sure boys only play in ways that are about violence, domination and combat. We take dolls away from them and ensure their play is removed from caring for someone's emotional and physical needs.' Michael says that boys are 'encouraged to perceive empathy as weak and feminine, and therefore something they should avoid'.

A capacity for empathy is one of the most integral requirements for all good teachers and carers, so it's no wonder that, until I was eleven and went to secondary school, I had been taught by precisely zero male teachers. The only male teacher the school employed was, predictably, the football coach. I'd never thought about that until I started researching this book, but perhaps that's because I was fortunate enough to have a strong male role model in my father. He made no secret of caring for me and my brothers, and he'd even take days off work to come and coach cricket at our school during the summer terms. Unlike the boys-only games on the football field, my dad's cricket sessions were for both boys and girls. For some of the children who attended these sessions, my dad was their only male interaction for the week. And for the young boys whose schools don't have a Mr 'call me Bill' Hemmings's cricket session, things haven't improved much in the years since.

Figures from the Department for Education show that only 15 per cent of primary school teachers are male, despite the increasingly desperate calls from many for this to change. Not only is the lack of male teachers a big problem for schools who are already struggling with a general teacher shortage, a recent study by the Open University concluded that there are now up to one million primary school children in the UK who, like me, almost reached adolescence having never been taught by a male teacher.

The lack of men within schools can cause a whole number of issues, particularly for young boys, as they look for a role model within their lives. When I attended a primary in Manchester for research some years ago, it became abundantly clear that the only male teacher, the now late Mr Brownridge, had become the de facto disciplinarian. That meant, rather than go to any of the female teachers, you were sent to the only man present in the school to be told off. This teaches both boys and girls that not only are men the ones who are truly in charge, but they are also meant to be feared. Mr Brownridge fulfilled the role, and thereby perpetuated the idea that a man is not someone you go to when you've got troubles – only when you're in trouble.

My mum worked in the school at the time and, speaking to her now, she describes how the school struggled to find a balance between care giver/teacher and disciplinarian for their only male member of staff. The school is in one of the poorest areas of the country and, at that time, over half of the pupils came from single parent homes. Mr Brownridge was used as a surrogate father figure for many kids, but a father needs to be much more than simply an enforcer of the rules.

In their book *Men Teaching Children* Dr Elizabeth Burn, a retired primary school teacher, and Doctor Simon Pratt Adams from Anglia Ruskin University highlight this very issue. In it, they suggest that talented male primary school teachers are being devalued because they get pigeon-holed into running sports lessons and are almost always responsible for looking after naughty kids. By assigning these roles exclusively to men, children will have a very narrow opinion over what a man's role is in their life and in the wider world.

The book also highlights the way in which men are far more likely to be fast-tracked through schools to become head teacher. This phenomenon, in turn, promotes the idea that men are better leaders than women, and are to be viewed and treated as their superiors.

While the statistics for primary schools are bad, it gets even worse when you skip back a few years to nursery teachers. In 2010 there were an estimated twenty-five male nursery teachers in the whole of the UK. Since then there have been numerous schemes to try to increase that number, such as the Men in Childcare scheme in Scotland, where just 4 per cent of nursery teachers are male, or the 'Bristol Men in Early Years Network' which has brought numbers up so that now 7 per cent of nursery teachers in Bristol are male. I'd recite more figures to outline the nationwide shortage of men employed in nurseries and primary schools, but, honestly, the numbers are so pitiful that I'd rather spare men the embarrassment on this occasion.

I spoke to one of the few male nursery teachers in the UK, Arkem Walton, about this problem and he outlined precisely why so few men join the profession and also why so many end up leaving. He told me that almost always being the only male adult in a nursery 'immediately makes you feel like an "other"', and that the lack of male peers means 'you start wondering if there is something wrong with you by choosing to work in this field'.

He says many of the men working in nurseries are often viewed suspiciously by parents, 'almost as if we're weird for choosing to work with young children', and knows of men who have been chased out of the profession by parents making unfounded accusations about their risk to children. It may go some way to explain why the rate of suicide among primary school teachers is nearly double the national average.

By casting men in nurseries as the bogeymen, it's hardly surprising that there's a fear of humiliation. This goes some way to explain why men, on the whole, are still reluctant to put themselves forward in these child-centric professions. And even when opportunities arise for men to take on a traditionally female role, it's seen by society as emasculating. Women make up 82 per cent of the care workforce and it's still ten women to one man when it comes to being a nurse. This fear of being ridiculed for stepping out of our gender-assigned role starts when we are little boys and we are taught to pay no attention to our own or other people's feelings. Some never overcome this emotional strangulation.

That mentality goes a long way to explain why, instead of encouraging fathers to be more hands-on with their children, we often mock their efforts and laugh at the idea of daddy day-care. A man alone with his children is still very much an anomaly. Too many of us still scoff and question why he has been left to look after his own child, while new dads complain that their employer actively discourages them from taking time off from their careers. If societal pressures aren't encouraging men to take an interest in the development of their own children, how can we possibly expect men to take on a broader role in educating other people's children?

So, despite UK government attempts to change the gender ratio of teachers in early years, 98 per cent of nursery teachers are still women. In no other public sector department is the imbalance so severe. When you consider this alongside the fact that very few male-heavy jobs include child care, that stay-at-home parents are nearly always female and that fathers account for only 10 per cent of single-parent homes, it's little wonder that boys can reach the age of eleven without ever really encountering a man. And zero men mean zero hands-on positive male role models.

Young boys desperately seek strong, male role models. Given how gender differences are still crammed into our subconscious at every corner, it makes sense that young men seek the influence of other men. Recognising the value society puts on a man, it follows that boys will always look to other men to learn how they should operate in the world.

There's plenty of research suggesting that the influence of a good quality nursery environment continues to be felt beyond childhood and into young manhood, and positive male role models have to become a part of that from the very beginning. A lack of men in learning environments is only going to show young boys education isn't a male domain.

This also means the concept of nurturing is one that, in the minds of young boys, becomes exclusively feminine. As each stage of their development passes with the guidance of caring women, boys will naturally begin to assume those behaviours just aren't expected of them.

Young boys therefore also don't see other men as a

potential confidant, and that's a dangerous path to go down in terms of their future mental health. Throughout these formative years, young boys are asking some of the biggest questions about themselves as they desperately try to understand where they will fit in to the world as they grow up. If there are no men around to help guide them through, how can we expect boys to develop with a well-rounded sense of self? If young boys don't get the chance to talk to men about how they feel as they grow and develop, why should we expect they'll do it when they're older? This is where we need to start making some serious changes.

I had the great privilege of speaking to the American documentary-maker Jennifer Siebel Newsom. Her first work, *Miss Representation*, which explored the way the media has significantly contributed to women being under-represented in positions of power, was extremely well received. She told me that as soon as it was released, many men began questioning why more wasn't done to examine masculinity across the US. She said she was constantly being asked, 'What about the boys?' or, 'Is there a boy crisis?' So, she embarked on a massive project and interviewed men from all walks of life to discover why, just like in the UK, American men are more likely to drink, commit crime, be violent and take their own life than women.

Her film *The Mask You Live In* critiques the definition of masculinity in modern America. As she explained to me, 'many teenage boys felt it was unnatural and uncomfortable to conform to the stereotypes, but ultimately they gave in'. In one particularly distressing scene, a male teacher asks the young boys to address whatever they've been bottling up. One boy, seemingly coming to terms with his emotions for the first time, breaks down. It turned out that he'd been the sole carer of his ill father, and hadn't felt able to discuss his personal turmoil with any of his peer group. The stigma attached to showing emotional weakness meant he simply couldn't bring himself to admit to what was going on at home, even to his closest friends.

During my own research, one group of five thirteen-year-olds told me they would NEVER speak to their male friends about their emotions. When I pushed them as to why this was, they said they feared friends would spread their problems around the school and they risked facing ridicule. They all said the only people within the school they could possibly open up to were female teachers – again confirming how young boys don't view other men or male authority figures as potential confidants.

Even more worryingly, they all also told me their fathers were off-limits when it came to admitting something as simple as 'feeling sad'. They all felt emotional discourse was a mother's job, again proving that men aren't able to converse openly and honestly with other men, even their own fathers.

Examples like these go to show how young boys shut themselves away from who they really are from a very early age. As Jennifer Siebel Newsom explains, 'they've donned a mask of masculinity and don't know who they really are or what they really love anymore'. All those things can have long-lasting implications for that all-important self-worth and emotional intelligence we'll all require in our later years as we attempt to face the world as an independent, free-thinking individual. But how can we expect to become truly independent and not continually focus ourselves on constantly impressing others when, from the moment we try to express ourselves, we're told it's undesirable?

The lack of men present during early years education also has an impact on the style of teaching young boys are receiving. Steve Devrell retired from primary school teaching in 2010 and says that male absence 'feminised this area of education'. This in itself is not all bad, but, when coupled with the fact there are very few male role models within schools, it may help to explain why boys are consistently underperforming in comparison with their female counterparts when it comes to exam results and desire to learn. Women are wiping the floor with men at the top levels of education, and the statistics that mark up this gender gap in education make for some fairly grim reading.

Girls are more likely to hit top grades in GCSEs and A levels. Despite the gap beginning to close as each year passes, we still have what the Higher Education Policy Institute described as a 'national scandal' when it comes to the university gender gap. They say men are less likely than women to go to British universities by as much as 35 per cent, and those who do go to university are 8 per cent more likely to drop out, while those managing to complete their degrees are less likely to get a 2:1 or above.

Each year, when the exam results come out and boys have fallen yet further behind, we hear the familiar growls of men lamenting the 'feminisation' of our education system. Instead of pointing the finger at 'the system' and blaming women for boys' failings, men need to start taking responsibility from the bottom up. We all need to take a second to really consider how many men took an active interest in young boys' intellectual well-being. I bet the number is low, like it was for me, and like it still is for a huge number of young boys growing up now. To combat this dire situation, men need to get more involved when it comes to what's best for the next generations.

In reality we need more male carers, more male teachers and more dads, like mine, who are willing to proactively engage with our early development. If nothing else, we need a balance between male and female care givers, so that nurseries and schools start to resemble the world beyond the playground gates. But unless men are prepared to accept the poor pay and the stigma associated with the work of those in professional child development, it will continue to be left to women – yet some men will still no doubt complain when the cycle is repeated for their sons.

CHAPTER FIVE

LAD CULTURE

After spending the first eleven years of their lives in a largely female-dominated environment, be it at home, at nursery or at primary school, we then pack our sons off to high school. Here, they'll spend the next five to seven years of their lives tackling not only their education, but also themselves and their peers, as puberty takes a firm grip.

When boys begin to reach puberty they consider, for the first time, tactile and emotional relationships with people outside their family. They begin to explore the world as a sexual being, and interpersonal relationships are at the centre of how their peer groups begin to form.

For young men there are difficult challenges that lie ahead, as those around them begin to grow and adjust to the adult world at different speeds. Late developers, like me, will wait with desperation for their voice to break, their muscles to grow and their spots to disappear. Those like my eldest brother, whose voice had broken before registration on day one, have a clear head start. By a coincidence of biological fortune, these guys are gifted with excellent sporting ability and the confidence to chat up girls knowing there's at least the smallest hedgerow growing in their trousers to be proud of.

All of those things lay the foundations for the emergence of laddish behaviour, as it's usually the more physically developed kids in schools who have the social kudos. Classroom intellect is rarely a springboard for popularity, and many young boys play down their intelligence in order to fit in with the rising rabble of testosterone-driven loutishness, peacocked by those desperate to assert their status as the alpha male.

It's another example of how traditional masculinity is to blame for young men consistently underperforming in exams in comparison with their female counterparts. It's that traditional, unchallenged idea of the alpha male, and the underlying belief that dominance is so important, that puts pressure on young boys to strive to fit in whatever the cost. When they can't, or simply refuse, the consequences can be devastating. Consider the suicide of fourteen-year-old Sam Abel in 2017. Sam killed himself after being relentlessly bullied for, among other things, his good grades. The barrage of name-calling, pranks and physical abuse he suffered pushed him in to a depression he never recovered from.

Bids for masculine dominance in schools can take many different forms, ranging from piss-taking and threats of violence to a more intelligent and verbal method of undermining others. Any schoolboy who dares to challenge the status quo is derided as an outsider by the rest and gradually pushed away by their peers. Those who remain in the inner circle spur each other on to do provocative and unkind things, all in the desperate attempt not to be shunned by the group – and so lad culture is born. And, as I said earlier, I believe lad culture, in its many guises, is to blame for almost all the issues facing men today.

Almost all men enjoy the adulation of other men. This breeds an environment within groups of young lads wherein each individual acts according to the will of the pack. This, in turn, means individualism is an increasingly distant concept to many young men. Interestingly, one of the themes I've noticed throughout the course of my research is that many men, whether directly or indirectly, talk of homogeneity when it comes to dealing with other men. It's the fear of the pack mentality that means those who disagree with what's going on are silenced by an overarching desire to fit in, rather than do the right thing. There's a real danger built into that notion, since without an acceptance of individuality, men don't feel able to challenge the actions of other men – and, as such, nothing ever changes.

One umbrella term that enforces maintaining the status quo is 'bro-code'. I'm sure you know what I'm talking about but, just in case, it's the belief in safety in numbers that allows men to act with impunity towards others.

I had the privilege of speaking to James McVey about this very issue. Not only is he a teen heartthrob and lead guitarist in the band The Vamps, but he's also now an ambassador to the United Nations' 'HeForShe' campaign, which aims to engage more young men in feminist and equality discourse. When I spoke to him about his school days, he told me that he and his fellow band members regularly considered giving up music when they were in their teens because other boys in their school bullied them about it.

'Even thinking about it now makes me nervous', he said. The problem for him was not only was he considered to be small and weak, he was also judged to be making 'girly music … songs about love'. His music was well received by many, including the girls at his school and other schools in the area, but, he says, the boys just couldn't allow him to have an easy ride.

The bullying didn't stop even when the band starting to become commercially successful. As the popular kids at his school and ones in the surrounding area got wind of his success, James says 'they were adamant to prove to me they were powerful and top of the hierarchy'. He felt so scared that, in the end, he gave up his education halfway through his final year only to return once the bullies had left.

This is a story played out at schools up and down the land. Like James and Sam Abel, anybody who dares to be a bit different or to step out of line in the eyes of the alpha males is often ostracised or targeted. It's all a continuation from the root cause of boys not understanding the concept of nurturing one another and the idea that men of all ages must fit into a specific mould.

When I asked groups of sixth form students what they thought made someone popular, the answers were fairly uniform. One common theme among them was how many girls you've got with.

Sexual prowess is another of those defining characteristics of masculinity, and considered something to brag about. While a man can prove his dominance as a 'shagger', however, women who sleep with numerous men are branded as sluts. While sexual desire among teenagers is no mystery, why are young men so keen to show off quantity of relationships rather than quality?

A friend of mine told me a story about how her father treated her and her brother completely differently when it came to sex. She explained how her father wouldn't allow her to close her bedroom door when she brought a boyfriend over, but her parents were more than happy to go out for the evening and leave her brother alone in the house with his girlfriend. How is it that men are more than happy for other men to have sex with as many people as possible, but they aren't OK with women to do the same? If men want to have lots of sex, surely it would make sense not to judge women for wanting to have sex with them?

What's worse is that one boy actually used the word 'conquered' when describing their sexual success. For a seventeen-year-old to see women as conquests points to the wider issue of sex being seen as a means of mastery and controlling women.

These boys also suggested that how much you can lift in

the gym and general physical strength is of utmost importance when it comes to the male hierarchy. The biggest and strongest boys are the school's top dogs, and don't take kindly to people like James McVey and their ability to impress in other ways.

Unfortunately, just like in our primary schools, there are too few men in secondary schools to call boys out on this behaviour and to set a proper example by encouraging those daring to be different.

I've already outlined the issues created by the lack of men in pre-schools and primary education, and those figures don't particularly improve as we move up through the secondary school years. What's even more alarming is that the number of male teachers in British secondary schools is now in sharp decline, dropping from one in four in 2010 to just one in five in 2016. Having missed out in their youngest years, these adolescents may even reach adulthood before coming into direct contact with a positive male role model.

So, along with the educational failure and lack of emotional support they've already suffered during their early years of education, teenage boys are then thrown into another environment where any possible positive male role models are slowly disappearing from view.

In addition to that, those masculine tropes have become so embedded in the collective male psyche that too few men beyond our schools are standing up to offer an alternative. So, with no other alternative available, young men inevitably turn to each other for guidance, or to the older boys in their school and beyond who have already suffered the damaging effects caused by a lack of positive male role models.

Sheldon Thomas is a former gang member who now runs Gangline, an organisation that works closely with young men affected by gang culture. While gangs may be an extreme example of lad culture in action, Sheldon pointed out to me how the vast majority of boys hoovered up by gangs come from fatherless homes. He says they're 'desperately seeking a positive male influence in their lives' and, without any alternative, 'they see the older gang members as father figures, and look up to them as their role models'.

Of course, the vast majority of teenage boys don't end up joining a gang as we know the word to mean, but it's common for rudderless young men to group together to create a safe environment for themselves. The sociologist Paul Wilson wrote that 'adolescent boys have a great need for emotion and affection'. Like usually attracts like, and so while those who seek refuge in groups gain a sense of belonging, they are generally looking in the wrong place for emotionally healthy male role models. These environments breed the most toxic forms of masculinity, spawning men completely at odds with their own feelings.

As I've already explained to you, I managed to allow myself to be sucked into lad culture by some of the most uber-masculine lads you could possibly imagine. Not only that, I craved their recognition. Their praise was like catnip. It was my primary focus from day one of university, having already adopted a similar disposition during my latter school days. I successfully ridded myself of any individuality and dumbed myself down in order to fit into the mould of a top lad, ready to do whatever it took to stay in the group.

Looking back, I ran with the pack and played the fool in a desperate attempt to feel some sort of belonging with a group of men I believed offered me sanctuary and acceptance. If it was that easy for me to adopt this fake, laddish persona, I despair at the thought of how hard it must be for other young men to avoid falling in to the same trap. From the Bullingdon Club burning £50 notes in front of homeless people, to university rugby players urinating on women, to the gangs of East London raping the girlfriends of their rivals, the all-too common denominator here is male dominance designed to impress other men. It doesn't take an expert to point out that these men, on their own, would be extremely unlikely to act in this way. But, be it through peer pressure or an inane desire to show off in front of mates, men allow themselves to behave like that without feeling the slightest bit of remorse.

While it's important to understand why certain individuals find themselves getting caught up with these awful actions, it's also a good idea to try and figure out why lad culture has become a part of everyday life for so many of us.

The issue men have faced over the past couple of decades is that, initially, laddish behaviour was encouraged. During the mid-1990s, with the rise of Britpop and the lad mags, the likes of Liam and Noel Gallagher were revered by almost everyone. As a ten-year-old growing up in Manchester, seeing those two council estate boys living it large and acting with utter impunity towards any form of authority was magical. They were the epitome of masculinity, and a far-cry from the camper male pin ups of the 1980s. The '90s indie boys did what they wanted, when they wanted, and were celebrated for doing just that.

Meanwhile, at the opposite end of the social spectrum, the high-flying city boys who'd began their cocaine-fuelled rampages in the 1980s also enjoyed a carte-blanche when it came to their behaviour. For them, it wasn't so much a 'fuck it' to authority, rather than a belief that they were untouchable. They were the crème de la crème of the lads with all the money, and therefore all the power. Both these groups may have represented a different brand of masculinity, but many of the founding principles remained the same.

That machismo swagger adopted by almost an entire generation went all but completely unchallenged for far too long, and men increasingly started to believe that they didn't have to answer to anyone. Then, over time, it began to evolve into something a whole lot more dangerous than a few bankers in Bentleys and lads in Adidas tracksuits drinking pints of Stella Artois sticking two fingers up to authority. Nowadays, we have pop stars and rappers living their entire lives as if the real world doesn't touch them. Grime and hip-hop artists still portray themselves as the pinnacle of masculinity and this, too, has become accepted by vast swathes of the younger generations. 'Guns, bitches and bling' may be a little absurd, but so many popular musicians call women 'hoes' that it's hardly surprising disrespecting women has become more mainstream. For those men, their masculinity is based on sleeping with numerous women, being dominant through threats of violence and proving their success through owning flashy jewellery and giant cars. They, and those they influence through their music and image, firmly believe that they are invincible and entitled to have their fun no matter what.

And if you think celebrities have no influence on lad culture, just look at the members of London School of Economics' rugby team who, in 2014, thought it perfectly acceptable to hand out leaflets calling female students 'slags' and 'mingers', all the while stating that their nearest rivals were 'scum who would one day work for us'.

• • •

Ever heard the excuse 'It's just banter'? This was, and frustratingly still is, the refrain of all who subscribe to lad culture. Any action excused as banter serves to normalise a sexist, homophobic and sneering mentality among the young men involved. In the case at LSE, the team was disbanded for the remainder of the year, but how often do these sorts of actions go unchallenged and unpunished at universities and beyond?

The word 'banter' was thrown around like confetti by my teammates at university. Some of them were studying engineering, others maths and sciences. On a one-to-one basis most of these guys were capable of having an intelligent conversation. And yet, en masse, they were virtually incoherent and awful. With no threat of ever being called out for our antics, we 'freshers' were encouraged to do some of those unspeakable things I told you about earlier – and it's a story that was being played out at campuses across the country.

When I arrived at university in 2008, the notoriety of club initiations had hit the headlines hard thanks, in part, to the advent of the camera phone.

The then president of the NUS Wes Streeting had already called for an outright ban on them after footage emerged of drunk Gloucester University 'freshers' with Tesco bags on their heads being led on a Nazi-style march through the streets by an older student, who was wearing a Nazi officer's uniform and a Swastika armband. In 2006, an eighteen-year-old golfer at an Exeter University initiation died after succumbing to what his father later described as 'societal pressure to drink beyond safe limits'.

Despite the reporting of these cases increasing in their frequency, my student union would gladly serve us pitcher after pitcher of cheap booze, such as snakebite, cider and lager, and even provided us with giant 'chunder buckets' for us to hurl into once we'd chinned our pints. Thing is, if this is just a bunch of men in a room drinking, then you could ask what damage is being done? If the men are locked away from the world, it's just harmless fun, right?

Well, no. Once a man reaches anything near the legal drinking age, peer pressure dictates that you must drink. As a teenager I remember being berated by some of my closest friends for simply not wanting to finish a beer. By the end of my first term at university, I came home so overweight I was almost unrecognisable to my friends. The older boys in the rugby club threatened social suicide if drinks were refused. One of the most popular games was called 'Next' and operated on the premise that as soon as you chinned your pint, the person standing next to you, and then the person standing next to them, and so on had to down theirs too. We sometimes played another game called 'drink until you chunder', of which there clearly weren't ever any winners. Sure, we should have been strong-willed enough to say no, but this isn't how lad culture works.

Serious drinking among men isn't just a means by which we can determine whom can drink who under the table. Part of its allure is that it temporarily reduces our social inhibitions. The drunk 'I love you, man' stereotype is a very real thing, and even those men who completely shun emotional connections find themselves being more open, honest and expressive about how they feel. Studies have shown that alcohol makes us feel more empathetic, trusting and generous, particularly towards those we already have a relationship with. This release feels good, and so we choose to drink more and more to prolong this sensation.

However, while certain levels of drinking can make us more relaxed and chatty, the more we drink the more it continues to affect the part of our brain in charge of decision making. Too much alcohol makes us more prone to aggression and we lose our ability to regulate our own behaviour. Social drinking with friends is a great way for us to form close bonds, but excessive drinking is also known to create a 'them and us' attitude between your friends and others. And as we already know, violence is a very male problem. Yes, women are violent, and yes, women sexually assault men, but I'm afraid the statistics simply don't lie. Men commit between 85 and 90 per cent of all violent crime in the UK, and nearly half of those incidents – over 1.2 million of them – occur when alcohol is involved. When lads get together and drink themselves into a stupor they then head out into the wider world with a head full of misplaced confidence and a pack mentality, and it's here that the real problems begin to emerge.

And it isn't just the damage done by excessive drinking that is a cause for concern by lad culture. The sense of dominance, whether alcohol-fuelled or not, within a big group of men is also a catalyst for men believing they are entitled to act with utter impunity towards other men, sexes, races and sexualities. Take, for example, the only time I can recall our rugby team being disciplined by the student union after some of my teammates took it upon themselves to insult members of an LGBT sports club on a night out. As a bizarre form of retribution, we were all forced to wear t-shirts bearing the ridiculously ill-thought-out slogan 'homophobia is gay' on our next club social. Instead of treating this as a serious punishment, the entire team dressed up in drag, got blind drunk and spent the whole night acting out homoerotic scenes to our great amusement.

The sociologist Michael Flood says that if we're to effectively challenge the behaviour within these groups, we need 'much more intensive intervention to shift those cultures with the view to gradually chip away at those norms'. He also highlighted university campuses as being particularly toxic places for women.

While lad culture is all about being accepted, the reality is that, for many young boys, the version of masculinity they're acting up to just doesn't fit with who they really are or would desperately love to be. Their true self is shut away behind a mask of bravado and, for some, that's where it will stay, possibly for the rest of their lives.

The author Jack Urwin told me much of the masculine behaviour he witnessed as a young man was 'performative'.

> When I've spoken to friends embedded in lad culture, it does usually come out that that's not really who they are. They're actually sensitive and have far more complexity than the person they present to the world might suggest they do. But for some reason, they prize this behaviour and it gives these men some social status.

And nothing epitomises the performative nature of lad culture more than the stag do. The stag do has always been a bastion of masculinity. Up and down the country and in the beach resorts of southern Europe, fancy-dress-clad men roam the streets, hump blow-up sheep and throw up their pints. It's all very much a competition to see who can get the most pissed, be the most ridiculous and make the stag look like the biggest twat.

The origin of the stag do is to offer the groom-to-be one last experience of 'freedom', before he's shackled to his 'ball and chain' for eternity. It means that, once the nuptials have been agreed upon, the groom becomes somehow emasculated, and the rest of his life is, in the eyes of his mates, lessened by the fact he has a wife. Now, I'm not at all against the stag do, but let's not think marriage represents emasculation.

Loving someone so much that you want to share your life with them is not a negative thing. That was, however, a belief firmly held within the university rugby culture. It was deemed completely anti-lad to choose to spend time with a female rather than with your teammates. There was no bigger sinner in the club than the one who didn't adhere to the rule. 'Bros before hoes' was replaced with the accusatory 'Bird-Gay'. To be with your 'bird' was somehow akin to being homosexual which, even now, I'm at a total loss to try and explain. Nor was it said merely in jest, either. There was no bigger sin within the club. To love anything other than the lads was to earn negative lad points, and to be avoided at all costs.

When 'the lads' see a bond, or the potential for one to develop, between one of their members and a girl, they jump to try and shame their friend out of it. While they make it look like you're being a 'shit lad', it's all about their own jealousy of you for finding something more meaningful than the often awful atmosphere that is their company.

Take, for example, the first man I met on arrival in Australia. I was renting a room off him, and within twenty minutes of my arrival at his house in Perth he'd already bragged to me about the number of women he'd slept with. Just like the school boys I interviewed, he felt his promiscuity was a base part of his masculinity, and something to be proud of. Then, within a day or two, and having met his girlfriend, his male friends began to lament 'how much time he was spending' with her.

I clearly bought into this notion, too. I didn't allow myself to enter into a relationship with a girl until after I'd dropped my facade of masculinity. When I lost my virginity, it took me all of five minutes to put on a dressing gown and go downstairs to boast about it to my friends. I showed no interest in the person I'd shared the experience with and chose to immediately show off about it instead.

As for the stag do, research claims to prove that the vast majority of men completely despise them. The study, carried out jointly by Madrid and Salford universities, suggests this is because men are pressured into doing things they don't enjoy so they can keep up with the other men and not lose face. Sounds familiar, right? Clearly, even men well out of their twenties still feel compelled to act up to the toxic rules of masculinity they've been brainwashed by.

We've all been to stag dos where it's assumed the strip club is a must-visit. But this study showed most men don't like strip clubs, and that some of the denigrating rituals of stag dos are not only unenjoyable, but also dangerous.

I was recently invited to a stag do in which the emailed invite contained the line: 'The aim is to do something fun, with a general humiliation of the groom.' So, a good friend of mine will be ritually humiliated by his friends while being forced to drink enough beer that he'll no doubt end up barely remembering his own stag do. Great.

Just to prove yet another theory, about how the cycle doesn't stop because nobody dares to question or say no, one of the first respondents to the invite 'replied all' with a triumphant comment: 'finally a chance for revenge!' What that revenge is for I simply don't know, but the fact somebody's immediate reaction to being invited on a stag do is to celebrate a chance for 'revenge' can only mean he's suffered humiliation in the past. And so the cycle goes on.

Why do groups of men think they have a free pass to act however they please just because one of them is getting married? Simply because they feel entitled to. Over the past few years there's actually been a growing trend to call out this behaviour. Beyond the studies that prove men hate stag dos, there's also more anecdotal evidence that both men and women are no longer willing to put up with it. Think about the uproar when the Ryanair flight from Luton to Slovakia had to be diverted in February 2016 because some men on a stag do got extremely aggressive and one even exposed himself to an air stewardess. They made the national press, and while some people cheered in delight at their behaviour, most people called it out for what it is: thoughtless men acting with impunity and entitlement with no thought of how their behaviour would impact others on the flight.

Sky News hosted a debate about the issue of stag dos and I was fascinated by the reaction of the former editor of *Loaded* (one of the bestselling lad mags of the '90s), Martin Daubney. He described himself to me as someone who has been a 'spokesman for men' for a long time and seemed furious that the traditional chaos of the stag do might be disappearing. He said the antics of men on stag dos were being watered down because of a fear of a 'digital footprint being left behind'. He also said stags were 'the last place men were allowed to be old-fashioned'. Martin Daubney is like many others who don't understand, or care about, the impact their behaviour can have on other people; although he did once admit that his boorish lad mag may have been the catalyst for a generation of men who've become regular users of pornography – something I'll discuss in more detail in the next chapter.

I'm really fortunate that social media wasn't around during my uni days. If it was, I'd certainly have been caught out and would have curtailed my actions a lot sooner than I did. I wouldn't have wanted my mum to see what I was doing (had she known the reality of my uni life, she now says she'd have brought me straight home), let alone the entire world. So, if the fear of a Twitter storm is inhibiting men from going on destructive rampages in European cities, this can only be a good thing. The fact they feel concerned about their actions going viral only serves to prove that they know they shouldn't be acting that way in the first place.

In a recent *Guardian* article questioning whether you can have a hen do and still be a feminist (err... yes), it was suggested that there was now a growing trend for 'sten parties', whereby bride and groom host a party together. In the ever-fascinating comments section, one man wrote: 'I guarantee this wasn't the stag's idea', as if the men agreeing to a 'sten party' were doing so under duress. One user's simple response to that was: 'Some men actually like women.' Well said.

The growing trend for mixed-gender stags is still resisted by some and it comes, of course, with an undertone of misogyny and resentment that the boys' club is being broken up. As an example, a colleague recently invited two girls to his stag and explained how, in the lead up to it, there was a WhatsApp group created for all the participants. Then, there was a separate one made from which the women had been excluded.

The only reason for this second group's existence, it seemed, was to be a talking shop for ladness. Memes, naked photos and suggestions of all the disgusting plans they had for the groom-to-be abounded. The other group was the place of organisation and semi-serious planning.

I can only assume that some of the men in the party felt their chat in the 'lads only' group was not suitable for the delicate eyes of the females. If that was the case, it not only points to a seriously outdated gender discrimination in the lads participating, but also suggests they would have been embarrassed had the women seen what they were sending to each other.

Perhaps inviting women to a stag do is an effort to dilute the rampant ladness expected of those in attendance. It certainly has had that effect on the mixed-gender stags I've been on. Or, and perish the thought, maybe the guy just has some close female friends and wants them to share in his joy, and the toning down of the laddishness is just a glorious by-product. Either way, it proves that the behaviour of men changes greatly when women are present, and that the exclusive boys' club is a very real thing.

Before you get upset with me for suggesting that stag dos should be banished to the past, re-read what I've written. At no point have I suggested that the tradition should end, nor that it is in some way a bad thing. All I'm suggesting is that it's okay for a stag do to not involve tying the naked groom to a lamppost, it's okay for it to not involve a trip to the cells or A&E, and it it's perfectly okay for it to include women, because they can be our close friends too.

What's more, there has to be an acceptance by more men that they can no longer behave the way their predecessors did for so long. We have to allow men to speak out against whatever things they don't feel comfortable doing. Nothing will change within the pack mentality if men don't have the courage to break the cycle, and nobody will have that courage if nobody says anything about how pressured we all feel to fit into the masculine mould.

We need to mobilise younger men and women to continue calling out these behaviours and to no longer accept 'banter' as an excuse for being a dick.

CHAPTER SIX

SEX & CONSENT

Sexual consent is very much an issue of our time. As more people speak out against non-consensual sex and definitions of what sexual assault actually means continue to enter mainstream parlance, the 'blurred lines' Robin Thicke sang about are fortunately (and no thanks to him) becoming less blurry by the day.

More and more women are now voicing their outrage against the barrage of sexually aggressive men they encounter on a daily basis and are coming forward to tell the police about their negative experiences.

The big question men need to ask is this: if there isn't a 'rape culture' and if misogyny isn't real, why are more and more women coming forward with examples of sexism from their everyday lives? Why is the number of rapes reported in the UK at a record high? And why do a further 400,000-plus women report being sexually assaulted every single year?

In November 2015 the BBC published an article entitled

'Do People Know What Rape Is?' They showed twenty-four teenagers, twelve boys and twelve girls, a video of a scene at a party and were asked whether they thought rape had been committed. The article suggested 'their responses are revealing'. I'd suggest they were frightening.

This is the basic premise of the video: Tom used to go out with Gemma. They bump in to each other at a party. Gemma kisses some guy called Phil. Tom gets shitfaced and passes out in the kitchen. Gemma isn't so pissed, and makes a comfy bed for herself in the lounge.

Tom wakes up and wants a piece of comfy sofa action. Gemma says it's cool for him to get under the covers. **She insists she wants to sleep.**

Tom tells Gemma she's pretty, Gemma goes back to sleep. Tom moves slowly closer to her, puts his hand on the back of her head, then puts his penis in her mouth.

Hang on, he does what? Yep, he PUTS HIS PENIS IN HER MOUTH. Seriously, go and read the article for yourself. I've paraphrased as accurately as possible and that's honestly what it says.

Of the twenty-four teenagers who were asked whether Gemma had consented, only 53 per cent said no. That means just under half aren't sure if sticking a cock down a slightly drunk sleeping girl's throat is consensual, and that is staggeringly awful.

Their responses range from the idiotic, such as it being a matter of 'miscommunication' (she insisted she wanted to go to sleep, and at NO point said 'please put your penis in my mouth'), the fact she hadn't explicitly said 'no' (she certainly hadn't said yes), to the distressing: 'We've all been in a situation with a boy trying to force himself on us – in the end you just kind of say "OK, fine whatever"', which is just depressingly dreadful.

How have we got to a point where a girl being a reluctant participant in sex has become accepted as normal? Or where the prevailing attitude of 17–18-year-olds means nearly half of them can't recognise that Tom clearly raped Gemma?

What's happened is that, for far too long, men's actions towards women, much like their general behaviour, have gone unchallenged. Nobody has taught these young people about consent, and it starts at a far lower level than what Tom did.

Remember the video of that girl walking through New York in 2014? The one where, in the space of just a few hours, hundreds of men cat called, wolf whistled and shouted their crude sexual advances at her?

At the time that video was released there was a deafening barrage of men suggesting this wasn't like them and the #NotAllMen brigade mobilised with force against it. Alongside that were the men, and some women if I'm honest, suggesting she was either 'asking for it' somehow, or that she should 'learn to take a compliment'. Sure, it's not as awful as Tom and his horribly entitled penis, but these men on the streets of New York all felt entitled to shout whatever leery comments they liked with no fear of reprisal. Despite the thousands of men in the comments trying to distance themselves from that behaviour, there's not a single example in that video of another man who was willing to speak up and say something is wrong the moment a comment was shouted. When this happens on the streets around us, honestly, do any of us ever speak up against it?

Fast-forward almost exactly two years and another video was released that shocked the world, and it brought misogyny and rape culture to the forefront of the global news agenda. This time, though, it wasn't a recreated story about an opportunistic teenager or the real-life fleeting squawks of men on the streets of New York City. No. This time it was the man who all-but owns those streets: Donald Trump.

The video was released in a desperate, yet futile, attempt to derail his presidential campaign, but the soon-to-be forty-fifth President of the United States was recorded bragging about how he grabbed women 'by the pussy' with all impunity you could possibly imagine. Whether or not he ever did grab young women by the pussy is almost irrelevant – though many have now come forward to suggest these weren't just 'braggadocious' words, as he would say, but a horrific statement of fact. The reality is that a man who openly talks to other men about sexually assaulting women is now the most powerful man in the world, and that sends an extremely dangerous message to everyone in the world.

In a terribly inadequate response to the outrage, Trump's contrition was offered with the caveat that his comment was made merely as part of male 'locker room' discourse. Discourse which also included the phrase, 'I moved on her like a bitch.'

Again, across the world, men rallied to try and distance themselves from the 'locker room', suggesting real chats in real locker rooms simply aren't like that. What all these people failed to recognise, once again, is that the locker room actually symbolises any space in which women aren't present. To suggest men don't act differently when women aren't around would be absurd, as proven by the secondary WhatsApp group ahead of my colleague's stag do.

When the 'Trump tapes' (as they became known) were released, there were a number of men who publicly condemned it. Be in no doubt that I'm delighted so many prominent politicians at home and in the US outright condemned his sentiments, but it was strange how many of the men did so under the umbrella of 'having a daughter'. 'I have a daughter myself', they'd say almost in unison, 'and I'd be horrified if that happened to her'. Sure you would. But wouldn't you be just as horrified if it happened to your mother? We all have one. What about your sister or cousin? Actually, scrap family altogether, aren't you utterly appalled by sexual assault as a whole?

You may point out that both these cases happened in America and that sort of behaviour simply isn't tolerated in the UK, but you'd be totally wrong. I'm living proof that the 'locker room' discourse exists. I lived it for two extreme years at university, only there that 'banter' regularly spilled out way beyond the confines of being 'men only'. Our words often turned into actions, so it's unsurprising many women subsequently came forward and accused Donald Trump of sexual assault. His British lapdog-in-chief Nigel Farage did nothing to suggest this awful revelation meant he wasn't fit for office and actually called him a 'silverback gorilla', as if his sexual aggression was something instinctive and to be admired.

•   •   •

In November 2016 a report by a committee of British MPs outlined the stark reality of where, in my view, these sorts of issues can lead to. In their own words, sexual abuse of girls in our schools has become an 'accepted part of everyday life' for many female pupils, and they consider that 'lad culture was to blame'.

The lead author of the report, Conservative MP Maria Miller, said that one in three schoolgirls now experiences some form of sexual abuse every year. That's a terribly upsetting statistic, but what makes it even more awful is that many teachers know that it's happening but admit to feeling almost powerless to do anything about it.

So rampant is the lad culture within our schools that not only are young boys lifting skirts, pinching bums and regularly calling their female classmates 'slags' or 'bitches', but the girls I spoke to say they have become numbed to it all. Take, for example, the testimony of one young girl I spoke to about this very issue. She's just fourteen years old and explained how, at her school, it was 'completely normal to get harassed'.

Sure, many of the older generation will say this 'happened in their day' or that 'boys will be boys', but these are both pathetic excuses to try and ignore what is a serious issue. It's that sort of flippant attitude that's led to a fourteen-year-old girl telling me that being inappropriately touched or spoken to by a boy against her will is 'normal', to a woman to be unable to walk down the streets without men shouting obscenities at her from car windows or to a sexist monstrosity of a man being elected to run one of the world's largest superpowers.

Despite these women and girls saying that they've become numbed to this sort of assault, the insidious nature of everyday sexism is clearly having an impact. Research carried out to promote 'End Violence Against Women & Girls Day' (that there needs to be such a day is alarming enough) found that three-quarters of women in the UK alter their usual behaviours for fear of harassment. These women told researchers that instances of cat-calling, lewd comments and groping have made them change how they would choose to live their life in an attempt to ward off unwanted attention and stay safe. Some even mentioned staying off work because of the way men at their office treated them.

I spoke to the model Kirstie Brittain about this. Just moments before we met, a man had pulled his car over to the side of the road and shouted sexually explicit comments at her. She laughed as she told the story, but also told me 'that sort of thing happens all the time'. She actually despaired for these men, calling them 'sad and pathetic', but the truth is those men will have driven off high-fiving each other for the verbal assault they just carried out. The attack totally under-mines the very humanity of their victim, reducing her to the status of prey to be hunted – but they don't think about that for a second.

Women have to deal with the unwanted attention of men far more regularly than many people would ever realise. You see it almost every time you get on public transport. An at-tractive girl gets on a bus or a train and there's more often than not a leery man blatantly staring at her, making her feel extremely uncomfortable. It happened just days before I wrote this when I was in the gym with my partner. As she worked out I saw a man very obviously staring at her. It clearly made her uncomfortable, but he didn't care. I asked if she wanted me to say something, but she said no and sighed, 'What's the point?'

And so, again, some will say 'she should take it as a com-pliment' or that 'there's no harm in looking', but looking is one thing, staring is another. For the man who stares in this manner, there has to be some form of gratification. Perhaps a brief glance from his target gives him immense joy, or the look of discomfort on her face affords him his feeling of power.

Take the testimony of Ellie Cosgrove in a piece she wrote for *The Guardian*. She talked of a man pressing his erection against her on a crowded tube while breathing heavily down her neck. Or what about a woman at the very start of 2017 who caught a man trying to film up her skirt? Now you may think these are rare occurrences, but there are over 1,000 reported sexual assaults on public transport every year – and those are just the ones that get reported.

It's blindingly obvious that sort of behaviour is totally unacceptable, but the question has to be asked as to why it's nearly always men acting in this sexually aggressive way? In reality it's because we're just not calling each other out when these behaviours start to emerge. It's because we don't realise the extent of the psychological damage our actions can have on other people. Nobody is telling men their actions could, and should, have consequences because, from as long as they've been acting that way, they never have.

We're now at risk of creating yet another generation of young people who've learned that boys' sexual aggression goes unchallenged, whereas girls have nobody on their side when they become the victim. As one sixteen-year-old girl told me, she's 'never heard of a boy in her school being punished for it'.

A twelve-year-old boy probably doesn't truly understand the severity of what he's doing when he casually pinches a girl's bum or lifts up her skirt, but he never will unless he is told, firmly, that it's not acceptable and that it has lasting consequences not only for him but, more importantly, for his victim. The longer it goes unchallenged, the longer it's perceived as an acceptable way to interact with the women he sees around him and those behaviours become normalised.

It also stems from those primary school days where boys are taught to suppress their emotions and feelings. If they aren't encouraged to empathise with their classmates as young boys, they will never understand the damage they can inflict on those around them as men. It's helps to explain why, as men get older, some of them feel entitled to their twisted pleasure and commit more serious forms of sexual assault.

Not only are some people still point-blank refusing to admit that there is a problem in this area, some go much further and even try to victim-blame women who have suffered the horror of being assaulted or raped. Women are constantly told they should not go out at night alone or that they shouldn't wear such revealing clothing or get drunk. But there's a much simpler solution to removing the threat of sexual assault: men need to stop harassing and raping women.

Unfortunately, when women do report sexual assault, not only are the conviction rates terrible across the entire world, the attitude of many men towards a male rapist is disgraceful. The most famous example of this is the case of Brock Turner. Brock gained notoriety after he was convicted of the sexual assault and attempted rape of a woman on his university campus in 2015. He was caught by two fellow students while on top of his unconscious victim and was there was no doubt he was guilty. But the story really became the centre of widespread and heated interest once he was handed a paltry sentence of six months (he only served three) by Judge Aaron Persky.

Despite the life-long pain Brock has inflicted upon a fellow student, his father deemed it acceptable to tell reporters that his son shouldn't have been jailed for just 'twenty minutes of action'. There's your male entitlement.

During the trial, Judge Persky thought it relevant to bring into consideration Brock's so-called promising swimming career and vocalised his concern about the impact prison may have on Brock. In fact, so concerned was the judge for Brock's wellbeing that, instead of sentencing him to fourteen years, as many deemed appropriate, Brock received a sentence of just a few months because a longer sentence would have 'a severe impact on him'. In the run-up to his sentencing, American newspapers also reported his swimming times and his athletic prowess. They even gave him the anodyne moniker of the 'Stanford Swimmer' when the 'Stanford Rapist' would have been more appropriate.

Brock's victim, meanwhile, penned and read to Brock one of the most powerful and devastatingly moving witness statements the American justice courts have seen. She opened her statement with the words: 'You don't know me, but you've been inside me, and that's why we're here today' and went on to go into breath-taking detail about the assault itself, its immediate aftermath (including exactly how the post-rape medical procedures were carried out), to the impact his attack and denial has had on her confidence to even go outside. She is now twenty-three and will suffer from the trauma Brock caused her for the rest of her life. He, meanwhile, is already out of prison and getting on with his life.

That Brock's ability to swim well was taken into consideration proves that society deems men's reputations as too important to be tainted by their decision to ruin somebody else's life.

There is, thankfully, a growing movement of men and women desperately striving to end violence and misogyny in all its many guises. Hundreds of charities, parliamentary committees and campaigns have been launched in the past few decades because women have simply had enough of being treated this way. Many men have taken heed of this, and there is no doubt that attitudes and awareness have been slowly changing.

The gradual demise of lad mags could have completely ended the warped objectification of women we are all bombarded with, but sadly that simply isn't the case. The exponential growth of sites such as the Lad Bible and UniLad carry the baton in the consumer race to normalise the sexualisation of women. In fact, the Lad Bible, which used to boast among its high-brow content 'Bumday Monday' and 'Cleavage Thursday', is now the twelfth most-read website in the UK. For years, sites like these uploaded feminist-baiting content alongside articles where you'd rate women's attractiveness. In fact, one article UniLad posted in 2012 ended with the sentence: 'and if the girl you've taken for a drink … won't spread for your head, think about this mathematical statistic: 85 per cent of rape cases go unreported. That seems to be fairly good odds.'

After the inevitable outrage that followed, UniLad shut down and rebranded itself. They now run articles about 'how to beat the bullies' and are trying to repent, but that doesn't mean they're off the hook. Websites like these that acted with such misogynistic impunity only a few years ago paved the way for the modern-day phenomenon of rape threats and rampant misogyny now ingrained across the entire breadth of social media – something that trickles alarmingly quickly into real life.

While it wasn't his purpose, the creepy arsehole who wrote that disgusting UniLad article actually highlighted an important issue – and the statistics are much worse than he stated. The conviction rate for rape in the UK is 5.7 per cent and that's part of the reason, as UniLad so succinctly put, that so many men think they can get away with it and so few women bother reporting it.

When discussing rape the men's rights brigade will suggest, as they will with all of these topics, that men are impacted, too. And yes, men are also the victims of rape. An appallingly large number of 12,000 men report having been raped every year in the UK. That number is too high, and we must work hard to try and bring it down. However, that figure is paltry when compared with the shocking 85,000 women who report the same violence.

Of course, some of those reports will be false accusations, and a very close friend of mine was once accused and dragged over the coals by police for weeks until the girl finally admitted she'd fabricated the whole story. But we cannot let incidents like that cloud what is clearly a real and mostly male problem.

Looking back over the annals of history, men have been

raping women for time immemorial, but the number of times rape is being reported has gone up 400 per cent in the past four years. So, either more men are doing it, more women are reporting it when it happens or, most likely, it's a combination of both these things.

It's quite easy to account for why more women are coming forward if you consider the hundreds of campaigns that have been undertaken to help them, but it's less straight-forward when you try to pinpoint why more men are now committing sexual assault than ever before.

Unfortunately for the youth of today, there is something widely available that is warping male minds when it comes to the way they view women, sexual desires and sexual encounters and it could go a long way to explain that rise in rapes: porn.

When I think back to the first days of my internet usage, I was stuck using a 56k dial-up modem. It took about five minutes for a picture to emerge on my screen. Line by line you'd see some hair, lips, top of breast ... nipple!!! Then somebody would call the house phone and all my teenage dreams would go limp.

As internet speeds increased, so too did the availability of the likes of LimeWire and streaming sites where, if you had enough patience and a few hours in which you knew nobody else would use the computer, you could just about download a three-minute sex video. As a fourteen-year-old virgin, I had no idea sex could last longer than three minutes. Little wonder then, when it came to engaging with a real, actual girl, my stamina was questionable at best.

I joke, but for many young boys internet pornography is now their gateway when it comes to learning about sex and relationships. I honestly believe I accidentally programmed myself to orgasm within three minutes or so because that's all I knew, so it's no surprise psychologists are becoming increasingly concerned by a generation with unfettered access to unlimited porn.

Porn is now not only accessible on laptops and desktops, it's easily streamable over 3G or 4G to our phones. Every one of us, no matter what age, has immediate access to sexually explicit videos whenever, wherever.

Since the advent of high-speed video streaming, porn use among men has risen almost out of control. The average age for first exposure among boys is now twelve. Young adolescents are now accessing pornographic content at an astonishingly early age and with extremely high frequency, with more than half of 11–16-year-olds reporting to have accessed sex videos.

It's fairly common sense, but plenty of studies have shown that exposure to sexual material from a young age is related to a propensity towards negative sexual behaviours. The content of these videos is damaging our collective perception of sex, as what we see on our screens becomes increasingly normalised in our minds. My generation and those coming after have grown up to expect frequent sex with perfectly proportioned porn-star-looking women. When that inevitably doesn't happen, serious problems can arise.

The amount of porn available now is off the charts. Any

possible sexual fantasy or desire, however lurid, is available at the click of a button. Over time our minds have become more and more desensitised to the sexual acts we see. We get bored watching simple one-on-one acts of vaginal intercourse as our brains have seen these images hundreds of times already. When there's no real-life stimulus to arouse us, our arousal levels drop and we search out a more extreme, far less common type of sex in order to get ourselves off. Once we're bored of that, we go in search of something new and exciting and we're offered a smorgasbord of sexual delights. It's why, according to the porn behemoth PornHub, searches for 'anal sex' increased by 120 per cent between 2009 and 2015. Couple that with research showing more than half of young boys believe the content they see in porn is a 'realistic depiction of sex' and that creates huge problems as boys begin to explore the real world of sexual relationships.

Knowing that anal sex scenes are increasingly popular with their consumer, the creators of pornography are, naturally, making more anal sex scenes. Then, as their audience gets tired of basic anal, the scenes becomes more violent and include double penetration or something more extreme to ensure their viewers remain aroused throughout.

The increased availability of increasingly violent anal sex scenes means more boys see violent anal intercourse as a natural part of sex, and explains why even the British government voiced concerns about 'an increasing number of young people engaging in anal intercourse'. Of course, anal sex can be a pleasurable and consensual sexual act, but it seems more young people are doing it because the porn they see makes them think that it's weird if they don't.

That same governmental report made a direct link between the 'unrealistic' expectations of young people and the increased use of pornography. And Michael Flood told me there have been numerous studies showing a direct link between the two, and that 'young people who use porn are more likely than any other youths to perpetrate sexual violence'.

When you then consider this in relation to the attitude of some girls who feel they have to give in to male sexual pressure, you're left wondering how many young girls have endured extremely painful anal sex solely as a result of male desire and not their own. It may also explain why a GP told me she was seeing a vast increase in the number of young women showing symptoms of violent anal sex such as fissures and even prolapses.

Karen Ingala Smith runs an anti-violence charity and she told me we should be extremely concerned about the ease of access to pornography 'because it's increasingly violent and degrading of women'. She says when you analyse the calls that are coming in to rape crisis centres, 'we can obviously see women reporting issues that are related to what men have seen in porn'.

I spoke to one father of an eleven-year-old boy who had bought his son a 'spy phone', as he called it, enabling him to view everything sent to and from the device. He was astonished to find his son receiving videos of rape scenes and worse from his friends.

Despite being pre-pubescent, these boys have already seen images of brutal gang rapes and horrific sexual violence – sent between friends as a form of entertainment.

Remember Nathan Matthews, the man convicted of murdering his stepsister, Becky Watts, in 2015? The last thing he watched before brutally attacking her was a video called 'teen virgin gets raped in her own house'. And during the investigation into 23-year-old Jamie Reynolds, who murdered a seventeen-year-old girl that same year, police found thousands of violent sexual images and videos on his computer.

Yes, these are extreme cases, but eleven-year-olds who are watching rape scenes implicitly dehumanise the women they see in the videos. This disturbs their opinion of the girls they see in the world around them and alters the way they interact with them. If they get sexual pleasure from watching women being assaulted, it's far more likely they'll try and re-enact what they've seen in real life to facilitate their own arousal.

As a result of this, men begin to recognise that they can use their sexuality to prove their dominance both over other men and, even more so, over women. If you want proof of that, you need only look at the dramatic increase in sexual violence used by gangs. Both police and charities have reported that male gangs now draw up 'sket lists'. On them are the names of girlfriends, sisters and cousins of rival gangs members. These are teenage girls who are seen as legitimate targets of sexual violence in order to mete out punishments, stoke rivalries between gangs and spread fear.

Clare Hubberstey, chief executive of the Safer London Foundation, said that gangs are using sexual violence 'in the same
way that they use dangerous dogs to parade their masculinity'.
She said that gang members know the consequences of being
caught carrying a weapon, and are using the measly rape conviction rate as a low-risk means of spreading fear and control.

Yes, this is again an extreme example of it, but imagine
how many sexually aggressive acts go unpunished every
day. Many men probably don't understand that what they're
doing could possibly be deemed unacceptable. Not only has
porn normalised it in their minds, the pressure on women
to give in to male sexual demands means it all becomes an
accepted part of sexual behaviours.

Male sexual gratification is now so easy that the appetite
for sex is growing. Many of us who've been brought up on a
diet of internet porn have unrealistic expectations of women
and become increasingly sexually frustrated when unable to
find a consenting sexual partner. That means men increasingly feel entitled to find pleasure whatever the cost, and
this puts women at risk, particularly with men who aren't
able to achieve it in a relationship or otherwise. That may
help to explain why it's now thought that as many as one in
ten men in the UK have been with a prostitute, and why the
most common clients visiting brothels are single men aged
between twenty-five and thirty-four.

I'm sure at some point in reading this someone from the
#NotAllMen brigade has muttered that 'women watch porn
too'. And it's true, a lot of women do watch porn, but nearly

80 per cent only ever watch 'soft porn'. Hardcore and violent porn in particular are very much male domains and are ever-increasing in both their availability and shock-factor.

Another problem created by excessive porn use by younger generations is that not only are some youngsters becoming desensitised to certain images, a fairly shocking number of school children admit to being addicted to it.

According to an NSPCC ChildLine survey, as many as one in ten 12–13-year-olds admits to having a porn addiction. A constant need to watch porn naturally leads to a totally reclusive lifestyle and, as sex and relationship expert Lucy Beresford told me, that has a huge impact on a boy's ability to create an emotional bond with a girl. 'You're watching it in your bedroom, alone on your laptop and you're not sharing that experience with anybody.' She explained how that easily leads to these boys making assumptions and about what they're seeing – 'and they may be hideously wrong'. Lucy says there's now a growing number of men becoming desensitised to normal sexual arousal and therefore beginning to act unnaturally when in situations with real women.

The women they see in the videos won't look like the girls in their schools, and so they will feel little sexual attraction or arousal when it comes to engaging in sex with their peers. They can also lose the ability to converse with the girls around them and they become ostracised – thus increasing their sexual frustration and their readiness to achieve pleasure via their hand and laptop.

Technology companies have started to recognise this

chronic isolation, and are quickly creating porn to suit demand. Three-dimensional porn, virtual reality porn and even sex robots are increasingly big business, but all those things only serve to further push men away from the realities of the world.

Catherine Mayer is a journalist and author of *Attack Of The 50 Ft. Woman*, and she told me that 'one of the features of the digital revolution has been to create ever-more ways in which it's possible to objectify and spread those images of objectification, particularly of women'. She's warning about the advancement of technology to aid sexual pleasure because it goes beyond the porn star willing to be degraded for sex. Instead she says men 'will find new and horrific ways of removing female agency' when it comes to attaining their pleasure, and it's easy to see where the danger lies.

Sure it might allow a man to experience sexual pleasure, but it is the literal dehumanisation of women in a sexual scenario. You only need to Google 'man kills woman for rejecting him' to see just how prevalent this issue is not just in the UK, but across the world.

Young boys' porn usage needs to be actively engaged with and discussed in schools before we end up with thousands of young men so desperate for sexual gratification they end up shunning tangible human connections or, worse, opting for outlets of extreme sexual violence. I don't suppose it will be the simplest task to undertake, but the fact that so few people in schools have been talking to youngsters about the porn they're watching points to a much wider issue within our education system and a nationwide failing of our young people.

•   •   •

A relatively new phenomenon that has arisen in our camera phone age is that of sexting. Peter Wanless, the head of the NSPCC, says that 'sexting is increasingly a feature of adolescent relationships' and that it is almost 'becoming the norm' for young people in a relationship to share explicit images of themselves.

It's now thought as many as 40 per cent of teenagers have taken a photo of this nature and there are a wide range of problems created when they do. First of all, if they are under the age of eighteen, any person who receives that footage is in possession of child pornography and is breaking the law. Of course, some of these images are shared between boyfriends and girlfriends in schools and you may think that's fairly harmless, but if that photo is sent to anybody over the age of sixteen, they could easily be arrested and put on a sex offenders' register for the rest of their life.

In reality, what often happens is that these images are taken and sent to someone of a similar age in the peer group. While two fourteen-year-olds sending naked photos to each other isn't the end of the world, when the relationship inevitably breaks down and the jilted partner gleefully sends those images to friends, then we have a big problem. Once that image has left the confines of a relationship, there is no stopping it being passed around hundreds or thousands of people.

When it comes to the practice of sexting, the information I've received is fairly patchy. However, in the conversations I've had, it became apparent that girls felt far more pressured to send naked pictures than boys.

One fifteen-year-old girl told me that some boys actively lead girls on with no intention of ever forming a relationship with them. Instead, the boys try and convince the girl to send them a naked selfie only for it to be shared immediately among his peers. I've since learned that this is a trick known as 'snaking', and it is an increasing problem within schools.

When I asked some of the boys present why somebody might do that, they sheepishly admitted it was a good way to 'show off' and make you 'look like a big man', all the while protesting that they'd never done it themselves.

In a bid to counter these problems, the government introduced proposals in 2014 for all schools to teach the danger of sexting during IT lessons. Schools would teach pupils just how quickly a picture can spread to try to deter them. But, as the then Children's Commissioner Sue Berkowitz said, 'sexting is not an IT issue'. She added her voice to those calling for compulsory Sex and Relationship Education lessons which 'must cover things like sexting and use of mobile technology, as well as other issues such as consent and harassment'. And she was absolutely correct in making this call. Trying to scare teenagers into not doing something won't achieve a thing – instead, they need to be taught to understand why they feel the need to share these pictures in the first place. It would be helpful if they were taught how to recognise the signs that they, or their friends, may be being coerced into this horrible behaviour.

You may have noticed that I've mentioned the government a fair few times in this chapter, and with good reason. For years, successive governments refused to modernise when it came to teaching children about sex and consent. It took five separate committees of MPs highlighting major issues within society for any affirmative action to take place when finally, at the start of 2017, SRE lessons became compulsory in all state schools.

And it's not before time, either. Take me, for example. I'm thirty years old and not a single person in my life has ever shown me how to put a condom on. Seriously. Thirty years and the only person who's ever offered to help was a girl trying to spare me the embarrassment of my drunken 'which-way-does-it-go-on' fumbling.

Neither my parents nor anybody at my school ever offered the advice. I can only assume they each assumed the other would. My first introduction to sexual education came courtesy of a video in a biology lesson which featured a cartoon duck. I'm fairly confident that's also where it ended.

I was never taught about the myriad of issues that can arise during relationships or, for that matter, during sex. The only things we were taught about were STDs and pregnancies. At no point were we told that sex could be pleasurable, and we certainly weren't taught what a stable, healthy relationship looks like. That the sum total of my sex education could be crammed in to a thirty-minute animation is bad enough, but I was hitting adolescence sometime around the turn of the millennium. Despite all of the dangers that arise by not teaching young people about sexual health and the differences between consensual sex and abuse, our exalted MPs chose to keep us in the dark when it comes to changing attitudes towards sex. Indeed, there had been no major changes to sex education from the year 2000 to 2015; that's an entire generation of young people who have been failed. There have been millions of young boys and girls who've been failed in this area for too long and the law change couldn't have come a moment too soon.

The more vaguely titled PSHE (personal, social, health and economic) lessons were deemed 'crucial' by the then Education Minister Nicky Morgan in 2015, only to be followed by her refusal to make them statutory. Arguments about religious schools and parental consent for lessons were banded around, and these were viewed as excuse enough to kibosh the proposals. Thankfully Justine Greening saw fit to introduce the necessary legislation this year, but not without some caveats that really shouldn't exist.

It's now statutory that every single child from the age of four begins a programme of learning not just about the biology of sex, but also about consent and relationships. They'll be taught about the dangers of porn and sexting and will be given 'age-appropriate classes' all the way through until they are seventeen.

All of that is wonderful, but the law also allows parents to remove their child from the class if they want to. Religious schools will also have the option not to teach these sessions, too. Given how stifling religious teaching is when it comes to sex, I'd say that the sons and daughters of religious parents should be prioritised in this regard to ensure they aren't completely sexually ignorant by the time they reach adulthood.

What's more, at the establishments that now take the time out of the curriculum to try and impart some useful knowledge to their pupils, Ofsted suggests that 40 per cent of them are doing a pretty rubbish job.

That means, of the schools bothering to try and teach sexual education, two fifths are failing their pupils. When it comes to advice on sex and relationships, often no advice is better than bad advice, and this should also be addressed as a matter of urgency by the current government.

Lucy Emmerson is the co-ordinator of Sex Education Forum and one of the key influencers in the government's decision. She says sex education 'must begin in primary school and build year-on-year to enable young people to understand a wide spectrum of issues, including the difference between acceptable and abusive behaviour, consent and sexual health'.

Without the proper tools to understand what consensual behaviour is and what is coercive, or worse, young boys and girls can't speak up. They simply don't know what's right or wrong. For younger children, it might actually help them identify the behaviour of one of the adults in their lives as a sexual abuse.

It isn't just the responsibility of schools, though. We can't overlook the role parents must play in all of this and men have to take responsibility for actively engaging their sons in sexual education. We have to admit that there are a lot of youngsters in this country who have had little to no good quality sexual education, and it's up to us to help spread the word. We have to accept our sons are watching porn, and talk to them about what they see. When they start dating, it's imperative we let them know what a healthy relationship looks like.

Recognising the failings their generation has suffered, there is now a growing movement within universities to correct their lack of sexual education. Many higher education facilities now require their first year students to attend sexual consent workshops, aimed at teaching both men and women the acceptable boundaries of consensual sexual activities. Unsurprisingly, in a world where men aren't used to having their flaws laid bare, they've caused quite a stir both on campuses and beyond.

Before delving in to the mixed attitudes towards consent classes, it's probably a good idea to outline why so many universities felt it necessary to introduce them in the first place. It's clear from the reaction to the BBC story about fictitious Tom that consent, for too many youngsters, is a woolly issue when, really, it should be black and white. We also know that when it comes to sexual assault, women are by far the most likely victims, with men almost always being the perpetrators. You'd hope that educated young people would know better than to act in this way, but research carried out in 2015 found that 31 per cent of female students reported having been inappropriately touched or groped at some point during their first term at university. Even more alarmingly, an NUS report from 2016 stated one in five students had suffered 'some form of sexual harassment' within their first week.

Assuming you accept that there is a problem, you must therefore accept that consent classes are a good way of attempting to curb the actions of sexually aggressive, poorly educated young men. You would also assume that, when presented with statistics like these, nobody would bother questioning the necessity for a couple of lessons on what consent might mean.

Georgia Turner is the Women's Officer and runs the consent classes at King's College, Cambridge. She says that many of the young men arriving at university approach these classes with completely the wrong attitude, and even attempt to undermine their legitimacy. She told me that despite the classes being billed as 'compulsory', the university doesn't check up on who does and doesn't attend. If I had to guess, I'd suggest some of those who skip the classes probably think of their non-attendance as a badge of honour while they sit in pubs making crude jokes about the 'birds' they're going to 'shag this semester'. Some, I'm sure, also sit them out for what they believe to be properly thought-out conscientious reasons, but I fear their attitude is somewhat misguided.

Other men go a lot further than simply missing the classes. Some, like Warwick University student George Lawlor, are so offended by the idea of attending that they hold up signs saying 'This is not what a rapist looks like' and write articles on student websites documenting their disdain for consent classes. They claim they're being patronised or, worse, considered an assumed 'rapist-in-waiting'.

In his article, George writes that 'yes means yes, no means no'. He also says that 'it's really that simple. You'd think university students would get that much, but apparently the consent teachers don't have as high a regard for their peers as I do.'

Well, George and your like, you would 'think university students would get that much', but when 20 per cent of students report being sexually assaulted in their first seven days of university, it seems you're very much wrong.

I have no doubt that the majority of young men at university or not have a basic understanding of consensual sexual behaviour, but there is clearly far too many who don't. By attending these classes, somebody with a better grasp of consent (like George and his wholly enlightened self) can help to explain it to their less-enlightened peers, and they may also learn how to spot signs of coercive or predatory behaviour and may, one day, be in a position to intervene and prevent a sexual assault from happening.

The two Swedish students who spotted Brock Turner assaulting his unconscious peer behind a bin and chased after him as he ran away were hailed as heroes. The nationality of these heroes, Carl-Fredrik Arndt and Peter Jonsson, becomes extremely pertinent when you consider that comprehensive sex education has been compulsory in Sweden since 1956.

But in the UK, young men arrive at university and resist engaging in something that serves to benefit the entire student body. Consent classes can be seen as a form of herd immunity, vaccinating everyone against sexual assault. Much like vaccinations, it only takes a few people to listen to some pseudo-science and the whole herd is put at risk.

Rather than embracing something that may just help them develop their social skills, some men feel affronted and lash out at 'smug, righteous, intervention' from the 'feminist zealots' who are only attempting to make their own campus experience a little less terrifying. For men to ignore that point reflects badly on the lack of empathy instilled in us from an early age.

In other news, the government did choose to intervene in 2016 when it came to legislating against certain types of pornography. Hurray! Right? Well, in a bid to address the increasing desensitisation and porn-related problems facing many young men, the government introduced the Digital Economy Bill and deep within it was a clause that sums up male attitudes towards women when it comes to sex. It banned content including female ejaculation, spanking, fisting and any sight of menstrual blood.

It doesn't take a genius to spot that these are all aimed at curbing the agency of women in porn. And this is really telling when it comes to looking at male attitudes to women and sex.

In his book *Ways of Seeing*, John Berger said this about an artist who painted a picture of a naked woman looking in a mirror: 'You painted a naked woman because you enjoyed looking at her, put a mirror in her hand and you called the painting "Vanity", thus morally condemning the woman whose nakedness you had depicted for your own pleasure.'

In his analogy, it is the woman deemed to be in the wrong, despite the fact the artist is the one drawing her with no clothes on. John Berger's comment is reminiscent of the victim-shaming that goes on in debates over who is responsible for rape. Many suggest that a woman who wears a miniskirt is somehow 'fair game' for unwanted sexual advances, and that she – and not the man – is the only one at fault.

Remember the girl filmed giving blowjobs to twenty-four different men to win a bottle of champagne at a club in Magaluf in 2014? Sure, it wasn't her smartest move, particularly knowing full well that camera phones had been invented; but what struck me about that is how she was the only one demonised. Articles written at the time speak of a 'shameless girl' who was 'outed' after being conned into giving her identity up. Notice that the names of zero of the twenty-four men involved were ever released. Nor were there any headlines suggesting the men were at all to blame. They were all depicted as innocents who happened to be standing in a row with their penises out. Again, the press blames the woman and the men involved aren't called out even for a moment.

Transfer these themes to the British House of Commons where our MPs are so focused on the women pictured in pornography that they completely disregard the many disturbing male behaviours. The porn is mostly made by men, for men – but, again, it is the women who are viewed to be the nasty ones.

Here's the hypocrisy, though. A woman is no longer allowed to be seen squirting on to a partner, but it's deemed perfectly acceptable for fifty men to ejaculate on to a single woman. A woman isn't allowed to be spanked (which for some is a deeply erotic and pleasurable act), and yet there was absolutely no mention of rape scenes anywhere in this bill. They're still allowed, just so long as there's no spanking in them.

To make the point even clearer, a woman in a porn video is now only allowed four fingers inside her, but multiple-penis penetration hasn't been outlawed. A single hand inside a woman's vagina or anus is, apparently, much worse than her being ripped apart by numerous male appendages.

And then the kicker: menstrual blood. Despite it being the most natural of all things, it's now banned in British-made porn. The UK has now legislated that period blood is too disgusting to be seen on a video by anybody over the age of eighteen. That alone proves just how backwards this entire process is and it makes a mockery of parliamentary intervention when it comes to issues involving sexual practices.

• • •

I want to end this chapter with a cautionary tale that I think encapsulates a lot of what I've been talking about. Let's recall the case of the footballer Ched Evans who, having spent two and a half years in jail for the rape of a woman in a hotel room, appealed against his sentence and had it overturned.

The story goes that Ched's accomplice, Clayton Macdonald, texted him to say 'I've got a girl' and sent directions to a nearby hotel. In court, Evans said he arrived to find his friend having sex with her, at which point Macdonald asked the girl, 'Can my friend join in?' Both footballers claim the girl agreed, but when she woke up the following morning, naked, she had no recollection of how she'd ended up in the hotel room.

Now, the Court of Appeal acquitted Evans the second time around (Macdonald wasn't found guilty) so, by the letter of the law, what Ched Evans did that evening was not rape. However, what we can say is this: in court Evans admitted that he and the girl in question didn't speak a single word to each other throughout the entire ordeal. Not. One. Word. He came in to a hotel room, had sex with a drunk girl without even bothering to talk to her, and left through a fire door hoping the CCTV cameras wouldn't spot him and that he'd never see her again because, again in his words, he 'had a girlfriend'.

That, my friends, is male sexual entitlement to a tee: a complete lack of empathy towards a fellow human being and a lack of education about sexual consent all rolled up into one. These are the sort of problems that start and end with us.

CHAPTER SEVEN

VIOLENCE & ABUSE

There's a strange paradox at play when it comes to the way men have been brought up and their relationship with violence.

I remember at a very early age being taught that, when faced with the prospect of fighting, I should always be the bigger man and walk away from it. It's something young boys hear over and over again in their early life. The idea of being the 'bigger man' evokes the belief that those who don't fight are, in fact, superior in their masculinity as they don't have to prove their dominance physically. On the flip side, for others, being the bigger man requires an obvious show of so-called masculinity – and it's these men who often resort to violence to keep up appearances.

Think back to your school days; did anyone at your school ever ask who the 'hardest guy in the school' was? I bet they did. And how often did some of your mates get to the point of at least squaring up to each other? The threat of violence is often enough to make one side back off, but that's not a healthy outcome. Sure it's healthier than actually fighting, but it still promotes the idea that physical dominance is the way to resolve disputes.

And beyond the playground, grown men still champion physicality and the ability to fight. You see it in gyms up and down the land, and you see it celebrated all over our televisions. We still call the heavyweight champion of the world 'The Champ', as if he's the ultimate embodiment of manhood.

Not content with punching each other, mixed martial arts is growing in popularity. We celebrate one man's ability to almost kill another man, live and in front of millions of paying viewers. The rise of MMA came about because boxing was no longer seen as enough of a spectacle. Boxers had become master tacticians, and the fans grew bored of fights where rivals wouldn't punch each other 'enough'. Violence is so normalised to us that we not only lust for it on TV, but often resort to it ourselves without a second thought.

Michael Conroy works in schools 'talking to kids about all the things the curriculum doesn't cover, but should' and is an ambassador for the campaign, A Call to Men UK. As he rightly pointed out to me, there is no male violence gene, 'so it has to be down to conditioning'.

In his work speaking to young boys about their behaviour, Michael says he's now convinced by the idea that too many young boys aren't called out on low-level violence, particularly in schools, and that the 'boys will be boys' mentality is all too prevalent. He says when violent men go unchecked, they see a 'green light' for their behaviour and 'feed off a presumed tolerance of their actions by a culture that doesn't challenge the roots of it'.

When it comes to violent behaviour, I'm fortunately no expert. Long before I had my epiphany about the dark underside of masculinity, I'd already decided about the abject pointlessness of being a violent person.

I'm a fairly big guy and have, for most of my life, had floppy blond hair. You can come to your own conclusions as to why I was often singled out as a target for the lads out to prove how 'hard' they were. I'd never wanted to be violent in my life, and had to learn quickly how to talk my way out of confrontation.

But one night I let my anger get the better of me. I'd seen my brother do it on occasion; either having to defend himself or the one time he smacked some bloke who was hitting his girlfriend (the police rightly let my brother off without so much as a caution), but up until then I'd had an extremely long fuse – and still do to this day.

However, on this one occasion, at a club in my small home town, one man was clearly adamant he wanted a fight. No amount of persuasion could convince him otherwise.

It turned out I'd committed the cardinal sin of speaking to his girlfriend without his permission, and he was furious beyond reproach. I even tried to 'be the bigger man' and left the club, only for him to follow me outside. So, at the end of my tether and sick of being pushed and punched, I picked this guy up, chucked him onto a nearby taxi and threw a punch at his head.

What I hadn't accounted for, and in my naivety as a pacifist, was that he wouldn't just lie there and take it. Instead, my fist clanged down on the bonnet as he ducked out of the way and my knuckles basically shattered.

Since that day, I haven't so much as raised a fist to anybody, not only because the doctor told me my hand is now utterly useless as a weapon, but because I learned an instant lesson about what happens when you turn to violence as a solution. There are negative consequences.

Despite the threat of a bloody nose or even possible jail time, far too many men in the world resort to violence to try and solve a whole host of their issues. Us men are by far the biggest culprits and its effects are felt by everyone.

One glance at the UK's crime statistics paints a pretty sorry picture when it comes to who is the main architect of violence in Britain. According to data from the Ministry of Justice, there are now 800,000 'crimes against the person' (legal speak for violent crimes) every year. And, when it comes to a split between the sexes, let's not forget men now commit about nine out of every ten of them. That same number translates across the board, with men killing two women every single week in the UK and 90 per cent of convicted murderers being male. But we'll go into the reasons behind these gruesome statistics later.

• • •

Imagine, for a moment, that you turn on your television and are confronted with this shocking 'breaking news' story: 'Dozens of Russian and English football fans were arrested today after mass fighting erupted ahead of the Women's European Football Championships. Riot police and water cannon were used to control the hundreds of rival female fans fighting on the streets of Paris.'

You just wouldn't believe it, would you? And yet, back in the summer of 2016, violence erupted all over France and male football fans fought endlessly before, during and after their respective countries played each other in the European Championships.

We may have been appalled, but we weren't all that surprised. It goes without saying that the football hooliganism witnessed in the 1980s and 1990s has mostly disappeared, but that isn't to say football fans, or men in general, are no longer violent. You might say these incidents are something of a rarity, but police forces up and down the country are dealing with gang violence and drunken low-level street fighting as part of their daily routines. Millions of pounds are spent each year policing the streets of Britain in a determined effort to maintain the peace between brawling factions of men.

If you're the sort of person who genuinely believes young men aren't still fighting with regularity, try going out in Cardiff, Newcastle or Manchester or any of the smaller British towns and cities as a young man. I did, and I can assure you it often felt more difficult to avoid confrontation than it was to seek it out.

You may say that 'men have always been violent' and it's a 'part of what men are', but I actually take great umbrage at these excuses. They exonerate men from taking responsibility for their violent actions, and imply that men aren't making an active choice when it comes to their aggression.

The psychology behind why men in particular become violent are complex, but, as criminal lawyer Joseph Kotrie-Monson explained to me, 'the vast majority of male on male violence takes place on a Friday and Saturday night'. He says it's clear with many of his clients that they struggle through their week in a job that doesn't allow them a physical or emotional release (which probably isn't paying very much, either). 'They feel their life has a lack of meaning,' he says, 'and violence offers them a release.'

As if by magic, two excellent examples gained media attention during the time I was writing this chapter. First, there was a video taken at a Wetherspoon in Trowbridge, Wiltshire. The 'Horrific Mass Brawl', as many news outlets headlined it, involved dozens of men engaged in a frenzied fight.

According to witnesses, the violence escalated from a one-vs-one punch up and grew into almost 100 men in a scrum. There's absolutely no way all those men had a reason to be involved, but a fight broke out and they all clearly felt compelled to throw some punches.

As is the way in this modern world, the incident was filmed by numerous onlookers including Tommy Arkle, who described the scene (handily enough) as 'watching football hooligans going at each other'. He also added that he'd 'seen fights before, but never to that extent'. And that's just the point: of course Tommy has 'seen fights before'. He's a twenty-something-year-old man who likes to go out drinking in a small English town. It'd be almost impossible for him to have avoided a fight.

Again, you might be from the school of 'boys will be boys', and you may consider a bit of rough and tumble after some beers to be a natural part of growing up for young men. But while it is a part of life for many young men, it certainly doesn't have to be. Nor should it be in any way celebrated or accepted, as incidents such as the Wetherspoon's brawl have been.

Mass brawls don't happen all that often, but sporadic bouts of violent behaviour are all too common in men, and can sometimes have devastating consequences.

Take, for example, the second incident that came to my attention at the time of writing. A 31-year-old man named Trevor Timon was found guilty of manslaughter in early 2017 after he punched a man he'd never met or even spoken to before, and killed him. He was sentenced to six years in jail.

The all-too-familiar story goes that Timon saw a man – in this case thirty-year-old Oliver Dearlove – speaking to a group of women he happened to know. The court was told how the now-deceased Mr Dearlove was, apparently, doing nothing more than commenting on some pictures of one of the women's children. And that's it.

That was enough to make one man decide he had reason enough to charge up to another man and deliver a deadly punch to his head. I'm sure his intention wasn't to cause death but, sadly for all concerned, that's exactly what happened, as the force of the blow damaged the blood flow to Oliver's brain.

Prosecutor Anthony Orchard QC described the attack as 'unprovoked and senseless'. He told the court 'it appears to have been motivated by the defendant's perceived sense of grievance that Oliver Dearlove and two of his male friends were talking to a group of young women whom Trevor Timon, the defendant, knew'. Whereas I escaped relatively unscathed from the rage of the man who didn't like me talking to his girlfriend, Oliver sadly didn't.

For some strange reason, both those men, and many others like them every weekend, clearly felt their position as the dominant alpha male was threatened by another man conversing with 'their women'.

And here's where the masculinity comes into play. These men have clearly taken to heart the lessons society tries to force down our throats that male dominance is of the utmost importance and should be maintained at all costs. A man who feels so threatened by the simple act of another man conversing with his wife, girlfriend or female friends that he resorts to violence is clearly a toxic combination of being horribly insecure and of the mind-set that women are his personal property, not to be interacted with without his permission.

It is this mind-set that answers for the Crown Persecution Service's findings that, in 2015/16, 'rape, domestic abuse and sexual offences now account for 18.6 per cent of the CPS's total caseload and this figure has been increasing year-on-year'.

We've already discussed the reality of rape and sexual violence, but domestic violence accounted for a huge portion of those crimes, with more than 75,000 convictions – a record high.

While it's bad enough in the UK, UNICEF has labelled violence against women the 'worst human rights violation on the planet'. Indeed, figures from the World Bank state that it accounts for more female deaths and disabilities than cancer, malaria, traffic accidents or war.

Back at home, Chris Green is one of the men who recognised this problem early on. He's been a part of the White Ribbon Campaign UK for more than ten years, and has even won an OBE for his services to equality. When I asked what made him start campaigning, his answer was simple: 'When I heard that UNICEF line, I couldn't help but take notice.' And he has a point. When you think of all the atrocities UNICEF is faced with around the world on an annual basis, for it to single out violence against women and girls as its number one human rights issue should mean that we all take notice. The sad reality, however, is that we don't.

At the time I spoke to her, Polly Neate was leaving the charity Women's Aid after nearly four years as its CEO. Her continual focus throughout her leadership had been not only to help protect women and girls at risk of domestic violence, but also to try and counter the culture that leads to so many requiring assistance in the first place.

While she rightly laments the lack of provision for those at risk from a violent partner, she is convinced that 'the way we construct gender' is the biggest cause of male-on-female violence. She says having 'worked at the sharp end of male violence' for that long has given her a real insight in to its causes. Put simply, Polly says it's 'the attitude men have towards women'. She says it stems from a culture where 'misogynistic behaviour among young men and boys isn't called out' and too many men are programmed to believe they have the right to be dominant over the women in their lives.

At the core of violence against women lies the absurdly outdated belief that women are somehow subservient to men, and that their entire existence is centred on satisfying us however we see fit. Failure on their part to do as they're told by the man in their life is a perceived threat to the man's dominant position, and it's there that the controlling behaviour begins.

And rather than blame the culprits of domestic abuse, far too often criticism is levelled at the victims for not walking away. People ask, 'why doesn't she just leave him?' But the age of austerity has forced many councils to make cuts to their provisions, and one such area that has seen massive funding depletions is safe houses for women fleeing violent men. And even those who do manage to escape face the horrifying reality that more than half of women killed by a partner are murdered once they've finally built up the courage and resources to leave.

The case of Mustafa Bashir perfectly typified this institutionalised ignorance surrounding domestic abuse. Despite admitting in court to pouring bleach down his wife's throat, hitting her with a cricket bat and threatening to kill her, the judge suspended his eighteen-month prison sentence because he deemed his wife was 'intelligent' and therefore stated she was not a 'vulnerable person'. Citing her university degree and close group of friends, the male judge allowed Bashir to walk free from court. Attempted murder was reduced to Bashir having 'behavioural problems' and he was ordered to attend classes to curb his anger.

Domestic violence is, of course, an issue that mostly affects women. But I'm going to throw a bone to the men's rights brigade here and agree with them that men are also suffering horribly at the hands of their partners when it comes to domestic violence. Thirty men a year die as a result of abusive relationships. Again, I completely agree with men's rights advocates that there is a serious issue of disbelief and under-reporting when it comes to male victims of domestic violence, and not enough is done to try and protect men from abusive relationships. But if you think about how masculinity works, and how difficult it is for men to openly speak out about their issues, it's no wonder these men are terrified of admitting to being abused by a woman.

While thirty deaths a year is still thirty too many, and we should all support any campaign that helps to bring that number down, women are just not killing men in the same volume as men are killing women. There is no way of getting around the fact that men are by far the biggest perpetrators of domestic violence.

So what is it specifically about men that means a proportion of us aren't able to control our aggression, or simply choose not to? With almost all acts of violence there is something missing in the minds of those responsible that allows them to act with such reckless impunity. Remember how young boys in school aren't brought up to recognise and practise empathy? Well, violence is one of the products of how we socialise young boys. In his book *Zero Degrees of Empathy: A New Theory of Human Cruelty*, the Cambridge professor Simon Baron-Cohen argues that the less empathetic somebody is towards a fellow human being, the more capable they are of inflicting physical and psychological harm on others. Their lack of empathy enables them to detach their victim from a shared humanity and it becomes easier for them to be unfazed by their own actions.

If you'd like even more proof that violent men have little to no consideration for the impact their actions have on the victim, just take a look at a recent report from the homeless charity Shelter. They say that almost a third of the rough sleepers they spoke to said that they'd been physically assaulted within the space of a year. They also reported that one in ten had been urinated on.

Given that men make up by far and away the largest proportion of Britain's homeless population, plenty of British men don't seem to want to show any compassion whatsoever for people so down on their luck that they're sleeping on the streets. It's indicative of the lack of empathy instilled in the minds of some young men, who in these cases are choosing to prey on the most vulnerable in order to gain some form of masculine satisfaction.

It isn't always just down to the lack of encouragement to empathise as children, however. Young boys are actually more likely to suffer physical abuse than girls and that abuse is very likely to come from somebody they know.

Psychologists and sociologists agree that childhood exposure to violence, whether experienced directly or simply witnessed in their home, contributes massively to the likelihood of young boys (and girls) developing aggressive traits as they grow older.

Michael Salter is a sociologist at the University of Western Sydney and focuses heavily on preventing male violence. He explained the reason why so many more young male victims of abuse become violent compared with female victims in relation to masculinity. 'Young boys are fed lines from such an early age about how being a man means they're in charge, but when somebody physically or sexually abuses them, they instantly lose that sense of dominance.'

He told me many of the male survivors he's worked with talk of 'losing their masculine purity' after suffering physical or sexual abuse as a child. Given they've been raised in the antithesis of a healthy, emotionally stable environment, and have been heavily influenced by a toxic, dominant male, there's been no room in their life for vulnerability. That then feeds in to their masculine anxieties, which are a breeding ground for aggressive tendencies. When these emotionally crippled young men start dating and having families of their own, they know from experience that they can assert their dominance over their wife and children through violence, and thus the cycle is complete.

It's becoming increasingly clear that many countries have a serious problem with the prevalence of child sexual abuse. Child sexual abuse went unpunished in the UK for far too long. The true extent of the problem will probably never be known, but in 2015 there were over 1,400 men being investigated for historic child abuse offences. By then it had been three years since the Jimmy Savile revelations had finally come to light, and hundreds of men and women felt they could finally come forward and speak about their experiences. Savile had used his position as one of the most famous and powerful men in the country to frighten his victims into silence. Allegations either were not taken seriously or were covered up by an establishment full of men who allowed Savile and his network of enablers to continue destroying people's lives.

The extent of the abuse is still being unravelled. Since the Independent Inquiry into Child Sexual Abuse started in 2014, it has worked through four different chairs and has reported back on absolutely nothing. Some survivor groups have withdrawn support and some of its most senior members have walked away in frustration. The inquiry is focusing on some of the most powerful men in Britain, but the male corridors of power are refusing full access to the truth.

The charity ChildLine reported that men and women are almost equally likely to abuse an underage boy, whereas men are ten times more likely than a woman to abuse an underage girl. The NSPCC's figures are less specific, but suggest that only one in twenty sex offences against children are committed by women. While child sexual abuse may have problems along racial lines, it is a mostly male issue. While this is no excuse for the behaviour of the men who carry out these abuses, some of them no doubt had themselves been cruelly damaged by abusive elders and feel too much shame to talk about it. The shame is never resolved, and that's why they repeat patterns of coercive, controlling, sexually violent behaviour.

So, men are more likely to be violent towards other men and boys, and they're more likely to be violent towards women and girls. But let's not forget that men in the UK aged twenty to forty-nine are more likely to die from suicide than any other cause of death. While it's true that a similar number of men and women attempt suicide, far more men achieve their unfortunate goal. Ged Flynn is the CEO of Papyrus – the national charity for the prevention of young suicide – and he told me that 'suicide is the ultimate act of violence towards the self'. He accepts that while women are more likely to engage in what he describes as 'non-fatal behaviours', men's violence against the self is more likely to be fatal. 'There's something about murder in general that is more likely in men, but there's also something about murder of the self', he says.

We already know men don't ask often enough for help at any time in their lives, and often the pressure that's built up in their own mind can lead them to act out. Instead of seeking assistance beforehand, they enact a horribly violent death on themselves, perhaps ensuring they don't have to face the indignation of failure (that most unmanly of qualities).

• • •

How to we begin to explain these horrifying truths about men? According to many psychologists, including a team at the University of Georgia, there is a clear link between men, their sense of masculinity and violence. Dennis Reidy led the research and found that the odds of becoming violent increase in men who feel they embody masculine norms. While this is fairly obvious, another aspect of their research was far more enlightening: Reidy and his team discovered that the odds of being violent were even higher in men who were the antithesis of the masculine norms and had trouble accepting themselves as being less than the standardised version of 'manly'.

When I think back to the days when men would pick fights with me, it was very rarely anyone my own size. It was quite often a smaller man who clearly felt threatened by someone taller (I clearly didn't look hard enough for them to be frightened of me), and wanted to pick a fight to prove something to themselves and to others around them. To the likes of you and I, this is more commonly known as 'small man syndrome'.

Research has also shown that the men who buy into masculine construct are more likely to be homophobic. To those men, homosexual men are akin to being 'effeminate' and, as with anything 'female' or challenging, masculinity assumes it should be opposed. Men with masculine anxieties also believe more strongly in the natural superiority of men and are both more likely to support war and less likely to recognise sexual assault for what it is.

If you want a fairly obvious example of these issues in action, you need only look at Russia under the leadership of Vladimir Putin. The Russian President has acute small man syndrome and it infiltrates the entire nation. At 5ft 5in., he clearly wants the world to think he is an unstoppably powerful man. Aside from his annual calendar, including the infamous picture of him riding a horse with his shirt off, his actions (and in turn those of the Russian people) expose his insecurities. At the beginning of 2017 the Russian Duma voted in favour of a law that all-but decriminalises low-level domestic violence. Russia has extremely strict anti-homosexuality laws, but, unlike most other countries, they aren't directly linked to religion. Russia has undermined global stability by invading Ukraine and annexing Crimea. Putin's ministers cheered as Russian football hooligans battered rival fans in France. The list goes on.

Or look at the alt-right and the men's rights movements now dominating the political sphere in the United States and beyond. All those same insecurities are true of the vast swathes of white men who feel that centuries of dominance of the white man are under threat. Rather than embracing a more tolerant, open society, they've doubled down on the racism, misogyny and homophobia the more liberal world strives to stamp out. They refuse to accept anything other than the white, male orthodoxy of their countries – which is why they gave Donald Trump, the figurehead of all of these pitifully regressive values, a free pass after admitting he likes to sexually assault women. It's why they also vehemently oppose feminists, and view equality as a direct attack upon men.

Many commentators in the US suggest masculinity is almost at a breaking point. Between 2007 and 2017 there were hundreds of mass shooting, and more than 97 per cent of the shooters had one thing in common: they were male. Remember Elliot Rodger? After stabbing his two housemates and another man to death, he drove around his university campus as he carefully selected his next six victims (and fourteen others he injured) before shooting himself.

Rodger had uploaded videos to YouTube chronicling his catastrophic emotional state after apparently being rejected by women for the past eight years. In his chilling tapes, he even admitted that he was going to kill 'stuck-up, blondes … All those girls that I've desired so much, they would've all rejected me and looked down on me as an inferior man.' His sense of entitlement was so disproportionate that be believed he had a right to female attention, and when he couldn't get it he felt 'inferior' – thus proving his masculine anxiety. Rodger embodied almost all the masculine anxieties possible, and his reaction was to lash out in one defining moment. He not only wanted to exact revenge, he wanted to ensure everyone knew he had the power – even if only during the eight minutes of his killing spree.

Dr Finn McKay is a sociologist at the University of West England and has spent years focusing on male violence. She told me that the constant internal battle masculinity forces upon men all too often has an inevitable ending: 'No human can possibly be stoic, constantly dominant, take charge and lead their peers without it having an impact. Any moment of shame or belittlement can ruin them. It leads to a moment of weakness, and they take it out on people around them.' She also agreed that those failing to achieve their masculine goals suffer emotional trauma, as they're never truly content with who they are. Reidy's study also discovered that the feeling of not being 'man enough' is actually extremely dangerous. His research suggests that men who perceived themselves as less macho than they would like to be felt anxiety or tension as a result. The 'reported rates of assaults causing injury [are] 348 per cent higher' than they are for men who may have felt less macho but simply didn't care.

That explains why the likes of Trevor Timon and Elliot Rodger suddenly lash out when they feel they aren't getting all the things they feel entitled to as a man. As Finn explains, 'men are more likely to kill and turn to violence if their sense of being male is undermined, shamed or embarrassed'. She believes much of the world's violence would disappear if we removed masculine pressures from men as 'it mostly stems from the insecurities of men who feel they're constantly competing with each other'.

While Rodgers and Timon are frightening cases, there is an even more extreme and terrifying example of perverted masculine anxieties at large in the world today. Commentators regularly demonise the religion of Islam for the atrocities carried out in its name, but something that is rarely discussed is that almost every single terrorist, regardless of religion or political persuasion, is male. Islamic State is a prime example of a movement that hoovers up men with masculine anxieties. These men are lured with promises of power and women – something their masculinity determines they deserve – and are happy for thousands of innocent people to die in order to maintain the dominance. It goes without saying that the women of their caliphate are treated abominably, and it gets even worse for homosexuals, who are routinely thrown off buildings to their death.

Psychologists have long hypothesised about the reasons men are attracted to groups like Islamic State, and conclude that masculinity is often to blame. Many attackers are loners who watch excessive amounts of porn, or have a history of domestic violence and controlling behaviour. Boris Johnson summed it up well when he said:

> If you look at all the psychological profiling about bombers, they typically will look at porn [...] They will be very badly adjusted in their relations with women, and that is a symptom of their feeling of being failures and that the world is against them. They are not making it with girls and so they turn to other forms of spiritual comfort – which of course is no comfort. They are just young men in desperate need of self-esteem who do not have a particular mission in life, who feel that they are losers and this thing makes them feel strong – like winners.

• • •

Men are violent because their version of masculinity allows it and propels them to be violent in order to achieve their macho goals. For the men who feel they constantly have something to prove to themselves and their peers, their mental torment must be excruciating, and that pain is inflicted on those around them, be they innocent bystanders, friends or family. The only way forward is to promote a kinder, more tolerant version of masculinity; one which encourages men to be the bigger man in the true sense of the phrase.

The most revealing finding of Reidy's study was that when it comes to the men in the middle, the ones who have no propensity towards violence, there was a common theme: whatever shape or size a man was, if he hadn't appropriated any masculine stereotypes and felt no anxiety about his masculinity, the chances of him becoming violent are virtually nil. Yet, even those of us who don't enact violence aren't completely off the hook. We've all succumbed to the whims of masculinity at some point or another. We've all watched men fighting and laughed. We've all casually used misogynistic language. We may not have been violent, but we've helped normalise bad behaviour. We're all partially guilty.

We have to stop giving men a free pass by saying they 'lost their temper' or they have 'anger management issues'. For many this simply isn't true. As Michael Conroy says, in most cases 'violence isn't a loss of control, it's about exercising control'. Violence is too often a calculated act to coerce somebody to give in to their demands, knowing all-too-often it will go unpunished.

It's time we stopped creating environments where aggressive language and violent actions aren't challenged. We have to bring young boys up in homes where violence isn't a part of their lives, and where emotions are nurtured so that stress and anxiety can be discussed, rather than literally fought against. Redirecting our anger into healthy channels, such as communication and support networks, is a real strength in the new era of healthy masculinity.

CHAPTER EIGHT

WORK DOMINANCE

You're more than twice as likely to be the boss of a FTSE 100 company if you're called John than if you're a woman. I know that's a real slap-in-the-face way to start a chapter, but I feel it perfectly encapsulates how far we still have to go when it comes to gender equality in the workplace. At the last count, there were seventeen bosses called John and only seven women.

There are also more male MPs currently sitting in the House of Commons than there have been female MPs in the history of British politics. Indeed, only a third of our current Members of Parliament don't have a penis. If you're a man, you're still statistically fourteen times more likely to be a CEO of a Financial Times Stock Exchange 100 Index company than if you're female. And it's not just good news for the boys at the top. Despite the Equal Pay Act now being 45-years-old, pay discrepancies between male and female salaries range from anything between 13 and 24 per cent, depending on whose statistics you believe. Either way, it's clear that the injustice is still rife. Over the course of our working lives, the average man is likely to earn about £300,000 more than a female colleague. Our Y chromosome somehow grants us access to the most visible positions in TV, radio and journalism, too.

It's undeniable that men still hold the highest positions in almost all influential professions. And yet, despite occupying so many positions of power and prestige, many men are still suffering from an existential crisis – so why is that? It's not often I resort to using Tony Montana, aka 'Scarface', as an aid to make my point, but nobody has explained the pursuit of riches more succinctly than he did back in 1983: 'You gotta make the money first. Then when you get the money, you get the power. Then when you get the power, then you get the women.'

There's something brutally truthful about that quote, don't you think? It's akin to the guns, bitches and bling trope I mentioned previously, and it lays down the linear structure some men perceive to be their route to happiness – and it all stems from a desire to appear dominant.

On my research visits to schools, it was hugely eye-opening to speak to teenagers of all socio-economic backgrounds and find out the answer to that all-important question, 'What do you want to be when you grow up?' I also asked them to try and think into the distant future to when they will be my age. I asked them to tell me what they thought success and/ or happiness would look like by the time they reached thirty. Almost all their answers had something to do with wealth.

For the boys at the private school, the answers were

drearily predictable: doctors, lawyers, accountants ... the suit-wearing list went on. The state school boys talked fancifully of being footballers, musicians or, to paraphrase a lot of them, just 'to have loads of money'. Very few of them were astute enough to consider that maybe a healthy bank balance might not be a guarantee of happiness. It just isn't a message society drums in to young men. Instead, as Tony Montana so eloquently put it, young boys are led to believe that the pick of the women and the wielding of power is the happy result of financial success, and there's very little out there to convince them otherwise.

When I decided to leave my job with Coca-Cola (an experience so hideous that I've already written extensively about it), it was an almost unfathomable decision to many members of my family. I distinctly remember my dad saying I was 'giving up a job for life' and all the additional benefits (a company car and pension) that came with it. To give up a well-paid, corporate career for the terrible money in journalism seemed daft to him, but to me it made perfect sense. One job made me well-off and miserable, the other made me worse-off but happy. And while I know that isn't a luxury available to every man in the country, by taking the pressure off men to earn loads of money we can allow ourselves to make life choices based on our desires, rather than external expectations. That desperate need for many of us to somehow prove our worth may go some of the way to explain why so many men work too hard and why the stresses related are now starting to show.

If you look at the education system in the UK, how-ever, it's little wonder that our perception of success is so single-minded. As every year passes, less importance is given to non-academic study and more emphasis is put on achiev-ing good grades in 'core subjects'. It all leads to the mentality that jobs, jobs and more jobs are the only things we must work towards.

Since the financial crash of 2008, wages in the UK have stagnated to an alarming degree. In fact, the Institute for Fiscal Studies suggests British workers haven't seen a real-terms wage growth in almost a decade, and probably won't see one of any note until 2021 at the very earliest.

In a society where almost 80 per cent of our economy is service based, the jobs market has changed beyond recogni-tion over the past thirty years; and, while older workers have seen small rises in real-terms pay and middle-aged workers have seen stagnation, guess whose income has been steadily dropping over the last decade? Yep, the under-thirties. So, who do we blame?

'IMMIGRANTS!'

No, sorry, I got a bit Brexity for a moment there, ignore that.

Actually, don't ignore it altogether, because buried deep inside the front pages of British tabloids screaming and pointing at 'others' and blaming them for our woes is a darker truth. The men who run the media and big business in this country are desperate for us to look the other way when they choose to slash salaries and decimate workforces, all the while paying themselves excessive bonuses and telling the poorer members of society they're simply either not trying hard enough or 'foreigners' are taking their jobs.

Take a closer look at the top echelons of industry and you can clearly understand why they'd prefer you not to notice what's really going on. As wages stagnate for us normal workers, CEO pay has continued to rise by nearly double the rate of their employees. It all means many of the young boys coming through our education systems, determined that they will have 'loads of money' or become mega-rich captains of industry, will quickly realise the jobs market they're entering isn't the guaranteed cash cow they expected it to be.

While actively choosing not to put immense pressure on our earning capability may be a luxury for some, market forces are taking those choices away from many men. Despite wealth and success being constantly thrown in our face as one of the benchmarks of manliness, the mostly male-run labour market is shafting the men caught up in it. I've already mentioned wage stagnation, but the issues facing men in the workplace go way beyond just that. In fact, the IFS also said twenty years ago only one in twenty men aged twenty-five to fifty-five worked part-time while earning low hourly wages. One in five of this group now find themselves in this position. On the flip-side of this, it now takes the average CEO of a FTSE 100 company (remember, most of whom are men) just four days to earn the equivalent annual salary of the average British worker.

Also, remember how I talked about male homogeneity when it comes to lad culture? Well, an almost identical mentality is having an impact on social mobility, and our male-dominated boardrooms simply don't care. In 2016 the Social Mobility Commission reported that 'candidates from poorer backgrounds' were missing out on jobs in the City because they dared to 'flout the dress code'. Some young men are genuinely being turned away from jobs they're more than qualified to do simply because they chose to wear brown shoes with their business suits. Alan Milburn, the Commission's chairman, said: 'Bright working-class kids are being systematically locked out of top jobs because they may not understand arcane culture rules.'

Men don't like a threat to their dominance. By hiring someone who is familiar to them, they feel more comfortable. It also helps to explain why so few women sit on the boards of companies, or why ethnic minorities are still grossly underrepresented in many influential jobs. I recall a story my brother told me when he went for a job interview years ago. On his CV he mentioned he'd played rugby to a fairly decent standard. Not-so-coincidentally, the man interviewing him also loved rugby. In all likelihood he was privately educated, too, and that immediately gave him the upper-hand not only over some of his male rivals, but also quite likely over all the women. While I'm sure he didn't get the job only because of this, it does show how much easier it is for men to get top jobs when other men hire the closest thing to what they see in the mirror.

The attitude displayed towards working-class men in top professions actually highlights a much broader issue that's plainly on view if you ever dare venture in to any of the top banks – and I did just that. As you walk around, you get a clear sense that there is certain 'sort' of person you have to be in order to fit in to these places. As I sloped in wearing trainers, jeans and a baggy shirt, I couldn't help but laugh as I was stared at, relentlessly, by men in suits. I was clearly an outsider. Maybe they thought I'd breached security and was attempting to subvert centuries of 'rules'. Or, maybe they just hadn't ever seen anyone inside their shiny phallic buildings daring not to play by them.

Similar rules exist within Britain's parliament. Astonishingly, it took until 2017 for the speaker of the House of Commons to finally decree that ties weren't a necessity for male MPs to speak in the chamber. But that didn't come without uproar from the old guard, who cried that the absence of a tie was somehow holding British democracy in contempt. The Liberal Democrat MP Tom Brake, however, stated: 'I think that if Parliament wants to be more representative I think if when all people see on television when they look at the chamber is men in dark suits then I don't think necessarily gives the right sort of diverse image.'

Of course, it isn't just men who suffer, either. Take the case of Nicola Thorp, a temporary receptionist who was sent home from her job at PricewaterhouseCoopers because she refused to wear high heels. Male bosses may think heels look good, but nobody should be forced to wear shoes that the College of Chiropody and Podiatry specifically recommends against.

This lack of tolerance for individuality in business creates a members' club, whereby those at the top ensure that anyone who wants to join their exclusive gang adheres to a prescribed set of standards. Just like the dominant lads who don't allow their authority to be questioned, anything other than deference to the whims of bosses results in exclusion. If you combine the fact that our economy is becoming increasingly service-based, and the fact that top-level service jobs are still being reserved almost exclusively for privileged men, you start to understand where a toxic culture within some professions can arise.

I spoke to Finn Toner who works in the City. He took it upon himself to become a mental health champion within his company and explained to me how the lad culture environment is very much a part of everyday life in these industries. 'In some offices', he said, 'the only woman to be seen is the secretary. With all those men together in a high pressure context, there is a constant pressure on you to perform.' And, just like men in any social or professional setting, Finn says 'any sign of weakness just isn't accepted'.

But the weakness he talks of in that context isn't professional weakness. It goes without saying that being poor at your job won't be tolerated, but what if your ability to perform is hampered by something other than your talent? What if you're struggling with more than just your job? What if you're actually struggling with your mind? With so many men around, it's nearly impossible to relay emotional distress to your peers, let alone your manager. In too many cases Finn says speaking openly about your emotions just isn't an option for men.

Geraint Anderson, a former City analyst and Cityboy columnist, describes the City as a 'testosterone-fuelled, macho' culture. 'The "lunch is for wimps" and "if you need a friend, get a dog" culture is just as strong now if not stronger', he says. And, again, the culture where somebody is allowed to stand up and say 'no more' doesn't exist either.

But it isn't just the high-flying city boys who adopt this mentality. It's apparent in almost any working environment where men dominate. That same atmosphere still exists to a certain extent in my profession, the media. In my conversations with older colleagues I've heard numerous stories of domineering and bullying on what used to be Fleet Street – where the old guard scream and shout at their underlings in part because 'that's how we were treated when we first started' – and it's undeniable that there's still an undercurrent of that idea running through some places.

These men can't handle the idea of a younger employee daring to question how things are done or to implement new ideals in to their environment. They refuse to accept that the working culture might change beneath them, and that you don't gain respect by barking orders (or by screaming 'you're the worst fucking excuse for a journalist I've ever come across' and slamming the phone down).

I was even dropped from the freelance roster of one sector of BBC local radio because, and I quote the Managing Editor here, 'it's not that we want "yes men", but...'

It's not only that sort of working environment that completely stifles creativity and individuality, but that atmosphere of fear represses any idea of changing work practices to be more inclusive and understanding of a more varied workforce. That lack of inclusivity is one of those driving factors behind uniformity, and a perceived necessity for uniformity is one of those masculine traits that can be so damaging to an individual stuck within it.

Given how many times this country has been through economic turmoil, it's shocking to think that 2011 was the first ever high-profile case of a top level CEO taking leave for a mental health problem. Antonio Horta-Osorio, chief executive of Lloyds Banking Group, was signed off work for medical reasons, reportedly stress and 'extreme fatigue'. But when you think of the culture that surrounded him, it's hardly surprising that he worked himself into a state of mental turmoil.

It's frightening to think how many men across all industries are pushing themselves to the absolute limit. Whether it's to prove something to themselves or to their peers, or because they feel the financial rewards on offer are the be all and end all, these people are often left with one escape route – quitting. For many of them, the thought of sticking at the job and suffering the stigma of their colleagues knowing they've had a mental health problem is far worse than being unemployed. That reality is the reason why men with a mental health condition only earn about 75 per cent of the average male salary. A diagnosable, treatable condition should not be a barrier to employment, but clearly it still is for many.

Instead, and as is slowly happening now, firms must rec-ognise that this is a serious issue and open up more spaces for men to vent their emotional exhausts – like Finn does in his company. I completely understand that by choosing to work in some environments you're signing up to long hours of high-intensity work. Hell, I couldn't do some of it. But that doesn't mean employers have no responsibility for the well-being of their staff.

If the men running these companies don't want to recognise the individual human impact the culture they proliferate can have, perhaps they should take note of the economic impact it could be having on their businesses. The Mental Health Foundation estimates that up to £100bn is wiped off Britain's economic output each year as a direct result of workers suffering mental health issues. Given that feelings of hopelessness are one of the precursors to suicide, it's not surprising that the Samaritans lists it as one of four main reasons for middle-aged men to take their own life.

Worryingly, research conducted by the Samaritans shows that there is 'overwhelming evidence of a strong link between socioeconomic disadvantage and suicidal behaviour'. Their re-search proved that men in the lowest social class, living in the most deprived areas, are 'up to ten times more at risk of suicide then those in the highest social class living in the most affluent areas'. Even the UK government admitted in 2016 that 'financial insecurity can be a big factor' when it comes to suicide rates.

There is now the same number of men working in the call centres of Britain as there were coal miners at the very height of the mining boom. As the volume of manual labour jobs decreases, so too do the sort of jobs working class men could step in to and feel they were still exuding a base form of masculinity. Jobs in the coal mines and steel mills of Britain offered a masculine sanctuary for those men who could return home each evening dirty, exhausted but proud of a day's hard graft. With the decline of manual labour, men like that have had to either adapt and find new areas of industry to work in or, what happens all too often as their age increases, join the ranks of the unemployed. Whichever way it goes, they find themselves in an alien environment and one that can have a devastatingly lasting impact on their mental wellbeing.

Towards the end of 2016 the BBC broadcast a show called *The Last of The Miners*, which focused on the remaining men working in the dying days of Kellingley Colliery, Britain's last coal mine. What struck me most about the men working there was the sense of belonging and the pride they took in their job. When the mine eventually closed, these men, some of whom were in their fifties, faced nothing but unemployment. The mental torment they suffered as they desperately searched for a new job was palpable, and the struggles they had in doing so made it a tough watch. But this is the reality in many of the working class areas of Britain now.

Those pressures exerted on men, by men, are also felt by many women working in top industries, too. The fact that men naturally seek to promote other men through the ranks of a company means many women say they regularly feel overlooked by their bosses when it comes to filling vacancies.

The Equal Pay Act was brought in to UK law in 1970 and yet, in 2017, the pay gap between men and women in full-time employment still stands at a staggering 13.5 per cent. Yes, it is falling, and yes, younger generations of women are now being paid almost as equally terribly as their male counterparts, but the fact remains that the average woman will, over their life-time, earn substantially less than the average man.

Now, there are those who suggest the pay gap is a 'feminist construct' or others who say the only reason it exists is 'because men work harder', but the stupidity of those people knows no bounds. The reality is that far too much of the structure of our workforce is set up by men to assist men, and women's needs seem to come way down the list of importance.

It used to be the case that women 'didn't want to work', or that's what the men would determine for them, at least. But now, as is being proven by test scores in schools and universities, women are proving they are just as, if not more, capable than we ever were.

Despite this, even those millennial women who have, on average, achieved over and above their male peers in education are still being slapped with an inferior salary. This is often down to them still being pushed into lower-paid careers or, even worse, being paid less money to do the same job as a man – which is illegal, but happens all the same. The Fawcett Society tells us that '80 per cent of the low paid care and leisure sector workers are female workers, while only 10 per cent of those in the better paid skilled trades are women'.

Sophie Walker is the leader of the Women's Equality Party, and explained to me why so few women make it onto the boards of big companies. Aside from the issue of motherhood – which I will discuss shortly – she recognises that 'the old white guys sitting in board rooms have one or two women on the board and somehow that means they're doing their bit'.

Thing is, I've spoken to numerous men on boards and, sadly, it seems that Sophie is absolutely spot on. Many of these men openly admit that one or two women are usually hired solely as a form of tokenism, and often against the will of those in seniority. And yet, having so few women in top positions makes it virtually impossible for men to be more directly involved with their children's lives and to take the time to care for their own emotional wellbeing.

Kathryn Nawrocki is the Gender Equality Director at the organisation Business in the Community and works with over 200 businesses throughout the UK. She told me that many businesses are now starting to adopt more equality-based practices, but she admitted it's 'very tiring, as many businesses just don't seem to care'. Rather than just hit these guys with extremely valid arguments for equality for its own sake, Nawrocki also pushes a business agenda alongside it, utilising years of research to show how companies with more diversity at all levels of management actually perform better. The European Commission suggested that EU countries need to get more women into the labour market if they are to meet their overall economic objectives, telling employers 'studies have shown that gender diversity pays off and companies with higher percentages of women on corporate boards perform better than those with all-male boards'. So equality in the workplace is beneficial for men, too.

In order to redress the male/female balance, many companies have now begun adopting quota policies for hiring – and, of course, Kathryn says many men are livid. 'There are plenty of people who are just towing the line [of fulfilling quotas] because they have to, but that's not necessarily a bad thing.' She, and many others, rightly point out that the current trend is promising, but goodwill alone won't suffice. 'The playing field won't level itself, so if it has to be fixed artificially, so be it.'

I recently entered a heated debate with one young (white, privately educated) graduate desperate to start a lucrative career with one of the 'Big Four' accountancy firms. As he slogged his way through the gruelling application process, he began to lament the fact that these firms now mostly had a 50/50 gendered hiring policy, and he was furious that he 'had to suffer' from what he considered to be discrimination.

His argument centred on the idea that he was somehow being punished for the failings of previous generations and that 'just wasn't fair'. What I tried to explain to him at the time, and what the feminist writer Sarah Ditum had explained to me in greater detail, is that men now believe women-only shortlists are sexist, but fail to recognise who has benefited from centuries of men-only shortlists, where women weren't even allowed to apply for jobs in the first place.

As Sarah explains, to suggest some positive discrimination in the opposite direction is somehow sexist is 'to ignore how societal structures have fought to keep women "in their place" for so many years'. Simply put, it means that a few men miss out on jobs. And these men see it as a massive affront to their sense of entitlement – and to them, that's just unacceptable. As for that graduate, I checked up a few months later and he had unsurprisingly got one of the jobs he desired; though, sadly, his attitude still hadn't changed.

In too many professions, the men at the top still see female colleagues as sexual objects. In September 2015 one incident that highlights this profound injustice went viral. Barrister Alexander Carter-Silk sent a message to a female junior barrister on LinkedIn. It read: 'Charlotte, delighted to connect. I appreciate that this is probably horrendously politically incorrect but that is a stunning picture!!! You definitely win the prize for best LinkedIn picture I have ever seen'. Tired of being judged on account of her appearance rather than her abilities as a legal professional, Charlotte Proudman tweeted a screenshot of the message with her own comment asking 'How many women @LinkedIn are contacted re physical appearance rather than prof skills?' She called out his 'unacceptable and misogynistic behaviour' before asking him to 'think twice before sending another woman (half your age) such a sexist message'.

When the backlash came, it was outrageous in its ferocity, and included rape and death threats. Men up and down the land once again waved the 'banter' baton, and suggested Carter-Silk was just a 'cheeky-chappie' who didn't deserve his private message to be shared with the entire world. There were, sadly, both women and men who spouted 'she should learn to take a compliment' narrative, but Proudman's stand was admirable. While the media circus around the story was often verging on the ridiculous, Proudman explained why she felt compelled to call somebody out and wrote that 'The eroticisation of women's physical appearance is a way of exercising power over women. It silences women's professional attributes as their physical appearance becomes the subject.' That the backlash against her was mostly male-led showed again how difficult men find it when someone dares to challenge their well-established male orthodoxy.

I've no doubt Mr Carter-Silk and his law chums had spent many years guffawing at 'totty' both in and out of the workplace, and not a single one of the chaps he socialised with had ever called it out. Instead, it once again fell to a woman to point out men's bad behaviour.

Another infamous cock-up in 2015 by a man demonstrates the toxicity of male dominance in the workplace. This time it was the turn of Nobel Laureate Sir Tim Hunt and his assertion that there were three reasons women were 'trouble' in laboratories. He was rightly forced to resign after telling the World Conference of Science Journalists that 'when they [women] are in the lab; you fall in love with them, they fall in love with you and when you criticise them, they cry'. He went on to suggest that there should be single-sex labs.

This is yet another example of a man unable to comprehend how men and women are equals. According to Hunt, when women are around, all anyone thinks about is sex. What he actually means by that is when women share a workspace with men, it's all men like him can do but to reduce them to objects of sexual desire.

What's more, he also highlights how emotional responses are unacceptable in the world of science. The mere fact a woman dares to 'cry' in one of his laboratories is grounds for permanently splitting up the sexes forever. FYI, it obviously fell to a woman to call him out over his comments. If this is the attitude of those at the very top of these professions, it only makes sense that it will have rubbed off on those joining the profession over the years.

And these attitudes are more prevalent than most of us would like to admit. A 2015 survey by *Stylist* magazine found that two in five women have been expected to make tea by their male equals and have endured sexist innuendos from colleagues. A third said they'd had their appearance commented on or had been accused of being 'pre-menstrual' if they dared to question a man, while a quarter have been joked about in a sexist way or patronised in meetings. Carol Glover suffers the ill-effects of a misogynistic work environment. She's one of the very few women working in engineering and told me the way she's treated by her male colleagues often makes her extremely uncomfortable. She says she often finds herself having to 'defend her choice of outfit' or being patronised by more junior, male colleagues.

And it's not just the women who are suffering this mistreatment. There are also a growing number of young men who also feel alienated by this masculine work culture. I had the pleasure of speaking to one man who works for the Highways Agency, building and maintaining our roads. He explained to me how almost the entire workforce is male, and while the camaraderie is something he really enjoys, what he doesn't enjoy is that he has to hide the fact he is homosexual from his colleagues. Understandably he didn't want to be named, but what he did want to make clear was that during his working day he has to present a facade while he cringes at the language used by so many of his colleagues. He knows that, were he to out himself or even suggest the atmosphere may not be inclusive for people like him, he would be ostracised, shouted down or worse.

And what about the successful banker who, at not even thirty, has already grown tired of the testosterone-fuelled world he is stuck in? That's true of a very good friend of mine who has worked tirelessly for years and, as he'd readily admit, embraced the culture within one of the world's most respected financial firms. He still networks heavily and allows himself to be dragged through strip clubs on a Friday night by his colleagues, but when I suggested stepping away from the nights out that he hates, he could only say that it's 'not that easy'.

Carol Glover also recognises this problem in her industry and laments the fact that at every engineering conference she attends, the 'networking sessions' are always centred around alcohol. She told me that being a young woman in a room full of increasingly tipsy men is a daunting experience, and far too often she becomes the target of sexual advances by her colleagues. She even overheard a male professor telling a young female graduate she 'wasn't networking hard enough', but when you consider she was faced with a room full of drunk blokes, it's hardly surprising she wasn't that keen.

These male-driven industries still aren't recognising the need for a more diverse workforce. It's becoming increasing clear that, as in so many different variations of its manifestations, when it comes to masculinity in the workplace, it simply isn't easy enough for men and women to say something is wrong, or to walk away.

That's something Sanam Gill understands all too well. She's a business strategy consultant and works with many big businesses across the UK to help them better understand the needs of their workforce. She's recognised that 'change doesn't happen because not enough people involved need it to change'. She's trying to get companies to adapt, but told me she's fighting against 'people becoming their clients, employees becoming their bosses and sons becoming their fathers'.

The longer those lessons go unchallenged, the more deeply engrained they become in the ever-homogenised workforce. Sanam says that's also why nobody has challenged the bland definitions of success. Given we've already accepted that many men of all ages define their own success and happiness based solely on income, or the ability to show off one's wealth, it stands to reason that men are finding it hard to universally redefine versions of so-called success and masculinity. But just how satisfying is it, really? The 'money can't buy you happiness' trope is longstanding, and yet too few men dare take it to heart.

• • •

In the same way we teach young boys which professions are 'correct' for them to aspire to, we do the same with young girls. Men just aren't doing their fair share of lower paid jobs because we're constantly told we have to earn the family bread. That not only stifles women's progress in the jobs market, but also limits men when it comes to the options they judge as being open to them: one of those options being childcare.

A massive factor of the immense pay gap suffered by women is female biology. Women have uteruses and, as a result, British society stipulates that the majority of the responsibility of childcare falls to them. We've all been there, inside a womb, but the system doesn't want to adapt to prevent women from being financially punished for bringing us in to the world.

Too many business structures are not set up to adequately deal with the fact that some members of their workforce are going to give birth. Take, for example, a Forbes poll of 737 women, all of whom have now left the tech industry. Of the 484 of them who cited 'motherhood' as their reason for leaving, only forty-two of those actually wanted to become stay-at-home mothers. The vast majority said that it wasn't motherhood alone that did it for their careers. Instead, it was the lack of flexible work arrangements available to them, the unsupportive male-dominated work environment or a maternity salary that was inadequate to pay for childcare that forced their hand. By feeling forced out of a job they didn't want to leave, it's likely to have had a detrimental effect on the future careers of these women. Naturally, their future salaries will have suffered, too.

The pay gap really starts to take its toll when women reach their forties. The pay discrepancy between men and women after the birth of their first child is somewhere just below 10 per cent, and ever after, it's nearly impossible for most women to reach anywhere near the levels of their male colleagues. By the time women return to the workplace having brought up numerous children the gap has widened to an almost insurmountable 33 per cent. The government's Department for Business, Innovation and Skills found that one in nine expectant mothers were dismissed, made redundant or treated so badly they felt they had to leave their job. Those findings led to the Equality Act of 2010, which outlined that any unfair treatment received as a result of pregnancy was an offence. And yet, still, the system is set up in such a way that women are expected to be the primary care givers and bear the brunt of the financial hit.

This archaic set up is the primary reason there's been only a 4 per cent uptake of the British government's shared parental leave scheme. The regulations, introduced in 2014, allowed couples to share fifty weeks of leave (thirty-seven of which would be paid) equally between them.

For many men, though, the very option of taking up that

offer is taken out of their hands. Despite the appallingly low number of men getting on board with the shared parental leave scheme, there is a movement towards more fathers wanting to be there during their children's early years. It's slowly becoming apparent that many men are more willing to put their careers on hold, take up part-time work and spend more time with their young family.

Every man who shows this initiative should be celebrated and supported (as should women who want to go back to work), but guess what? Business doesn't care. The ruthless money-makers show no concern for those men who dare to break away from the uniformity in their workplaces, and they make life as difficult as possible for these progressive fathers.

A recent study conducted by the University of Plymouth highlighted this hideously outdated attitude possessed by far too many employers when it comes to their male employees and their desire to be a present father. Remember how terrible the gender pay gap is for women? And how it gets even worse when they decide to have a child? Well, men also have their own pay gap. Honestly, they do. We know that men in full-time work are doing far better than their female colleagues when it comes to their take-home salary, but if a man decides to go part-time, somehow the financial systems see him as less valuable than his female counterpart and choose to punish him to the tune of an 11 per cent pay reduction. It's true. Men working part-time now earn far less than a woman who works part-time in the same job. This is something the Plymouth researchers described as the 'fatherhood forfeit'.

Matt Sharpe is a father who has suffered this exact fate and, in an excellent article in *The Independent*, he outlined precisely what wanting to be a hands-on father can do to your career. He wrote that:

> Within a few months of becoming a first-time father, trying to balance the new demands of a needy baby, sleepless nights and a job that currently didn't have all my focus, I was pulled aside by my manager – someone who had no children – and told that 'sometimes work needs to come before family'.

If this were the case for both men and women, who would be left at home? There would be no parent there for the baby.

Jasmine Kelland is a lecturer in Human Resources at Plymouth. She says that 'in the UK, traditional patterns of employment and parenting are in decline, and the stereotype of fathers going to work while mothers raise a family are increasingly diminishing.' She says data clearly shows an increasing number of fathers working fewer hours to accommodate family life, while mothers are more frequently working full-time.

Here we have solid indication that more and more families want the opportunity to share the burden when it comes to raising a family. Sadly, though, we also have evidence that the male-dominated business world isn't adapting its mentality to help the cause. As Jasmine says, 'a shift in the attitudes of employers is required so that workers are treated fairly on the basis of their skill set rather than their familial choices'.

And yet, despite these positively shifting trends, new mothers are afforded far more freedom when it comes to raising their family. Employers are more understanding when a female employee has to care for their sick child, pick them up from school or attend a parents' evening, but not so for men, and Matt Sharpe says he's now been 'let go' from jobs, felt himself plateauing and watched as men who haven't prioritised childcare or don't have children are promoted ahead of him.

We're now in a ludicrous situation where both men and women are being punished for wanting to raise their children. This state of affairs reinforces the archaic notion that women are care givers and men are breadwinners – and the crusty old suits at the top aren't allowing that ancient formula to change.

I recently spoke to a former colleague (who asked not to be named) about his experience of fatherhood within my profession. He told me that there was constant pushback from an all-male team of bosses when he asked for longer than the paltry two weeks of parental leave offered to new fathers. Here's what he told me: 'I was shocked to see how affronted they were by the idea I'd want to spend time with my son rather than come in to the office every day. They'd constantly ask "Where's your wife? What's your wife doing?"'

They didn't go quite as far as saying it directly, but they were insinuating that it was his wife's job to raise their son, not his. 'When I finally relented and gave in to them,' he said, 'they were still funny about me dropping to four days a week rather than five, even though my hours would stay the same.'

I fear that's the experience of too many men across the UK. The Fatherhood Institute lobbied hard for the new parental leave legislation and welcomed it as a step in the right direction. However, when the scheme was introduced, their spokesman Jeremy Davies said the main obstacle was cultural and 'employers have a job to do to transform the status quo'. He said male employees find it difficult to 'stand up and be counted' when it comes to taking leave and suggested that male-dominated industries are the worst offenders. The men at the top of the food-chain aren't giving allowances to a new generation of fathers who actually want to be more 'hands on'.

While that doesn't completely absolve individual men of responsibility for the shockingly low levels of us pulling our weight when it comes to child rearing (as many as 40 per cent of men still don't take any sort of parental leave), it does go a long way to explain why the uptake has been so slight.

When the Fatherhood Institute, whose entire raison d'être is to engender a 'father-inclusive approach' to policy, say that male-dominated industries are the worst offenders when it comes to stifling men taking parental leave, it becomes difficult to argue that this is not a male problem which requires a male solution.

CHAPTER NINE

THE MEDIA

Nobody could possibly predict at the beginning of 2016 that a self-confessed sexual aggressor would end up winning his place in the White House of America; but, given how that year started, we shouldn't have been surprised.

Gentleman's Quarterly, more commonly known by the abbreviated *GQ*, heralded the arrival of the new year by offering us three different magazine covers, all depicting the image of a different 'Man of the Year'. On one cover was Usain Bolt, 'World Dominator', with his suit jacket unfastened to show off his perfect abs. Next up was Ryan Reynolds, 'America's Suave Sophisticated Superhero' in a mottled blue dinner jacket and bowtie, designed to show off both his wealth and his perfect looks. And last but by no means least was Warren Beatty, 'The Original Hollywood Playboy' showing off nothing, but not needing to as *GQ* helpfully told us he'd slept with hundreds of women.

The third most-read men's magazine in the world kicked

off 2016 by promoting rampant masculinity as being the most desirable asset men could hope for. In their eyes, men worth celebrating must either have a sculpted body, be rich and good looking or have been a Lothario. As one *Guardian* journalist rightly pointed out: in 2016, 'the alpha male was back'.

But if the alpha was 'back', where had it been? Perhaps during the metrosexual years it had, at best, been on hiatus – but those traditional tropes hadn't been gone long, and certainly not long enough to have discouraged anyone from championing them once again.

I'm not saying *GQ* was directly responsible for President Trump, but what I am saying is that the depiction of these men, and the celebration of them as the pinnacle of manliness, is all part of the rich tapestry of masculinity that can, apparently, lead to an overt misogynist and a man many of his fans celebrate as an 'alpha male' becoming the most powerful man in the world.

Over the past 100 years or so, men have had at their disposal one of the most powerful influencers humanity has ever invented: the media. The media is everywhere and, from the movies we watch to the adverts we see on our commute to work, like it or not, it has an enormous impact on how we view ourselves and each other. The power of the media is strong. It's utilised by everyone from would-be tyrants (successful ones, too), global corporations and, increasingly, individuals in an attempt to boost their image and sell us an idealised version of themselves. That ideal can come in numerous forms, but the pervasive messaging we are fed can have a long-lasting and devastating impact on our psyches.

Traditionally, the biggest influencer when it comes to how us mere mortals judge ourselves has been the Big Screen. Hollywood movie stars are still among the most well-known celebrities in the world, and millions of people across the globe look up to these actors as their idols. It figures, then, that the clothes they wear, the products they endorse and the lifestyles they promote will gradually permeate throughout the real world. So, how is Hollywood doing when it comes to gender equality and promoting a healthy vision of how men and women alike should be behaving? Pretty badly, actually.

It doesn't get much better after the Disney princes and princesses we see as children. Most big budget blockbuster films contain a strong, tough leading man and a secondary female character that is most likely of romantic interest to our male hero.

You can correctly assume that in order to write complex, well-researched female roles, you need to hire a large number of astute female writers. It would also follow that, given 50 per cent of the world's population is female and movies are supposed to at least in some way mimic real life, at least 50 per cent of the characters in films would be female. Wrong and wrong again.

Of the top 250 grossing movies of 2015, about one in ten of the scriptwriters was female. As for women actually being on our screen, less than one quarter of leading roles were written for them, and you're twice as likely to see the female character take her clothes off than the male lead. With so many of the writers being male and men liking the idea of being talked about, it's hardly surprising that many of the female characters exist merely to serve men's egos.

In 1985 the cartoonist Alison Bechdel introduced the world to her 'rule' when it comes to movies. In one of her comic strips, a woman says she only goes to a movie if it contains more than one woman, they talk to each other and they're not just discussing men. According to the website bechdeltest.com, of the top 176 films released in 2016, sixty-one of them failed to fulfil one or more of these criteria.

You may say that's not significant, but the fact that Hollywood is still churning out more than a third of big budget movies wherein women either don't talk to each other, or only discuss the men in their lives, proves how far the industry still has to go when it comes to its standards of equality.

The situation has become so bad for actors that the performer's union Equity is now calling for specialist mental health care for its female members. At the Trade Union Congress Women's Conference in 2017, Equity put forward a motion stating that: 'Young women in particular are pressured to have "the right look" or to be "the right size" and to blend in with a body image that is deemed acceptable and that supposedly will help them succeed in their career.' Equity also highlighted the fact that female actors are now expected to do more nude scenes than ever before, and women in their thirties are considered too old to star alongside men almost twice their age.

Testimony from one of their members, RADA graduate Rosie Hilal, revealed how she is often made to hide 'any trace of her intelligence and capabilities as a human being' and notes that the 'body and beauty ideals are very often demeaning, even in the supposedly high end of movie making'.

The movies still have a long way to go when it comes to their portrayal of men, too. Keith Richman, the then-CEO of Break Media in the US, spoke to 2,000 18–49-year-olds to find out 'the state of being a man in 2012' and concluded that men feel they 'aren't being portrayed correctly'. He said the media industry 'has tended to characterise men as macho guys, skirt chasers and inept at parenting and relationships', and I'd hasten to add that very little has changed in the five years hence. These are some of the basic masculine tropes we're forced to grapple with from an early age, and the men we see on our screens are doing very little to counter that ongoing narrative.

Just tackling the superhero movie genre alone, in 2016 we were hit with *Deadpool*, *Batman vs Superman*, *Suicide Squad*, *Captain America*, *Doctor Strange* and *X-Men: Apocalypse* to name but a few. Production companies are cashing in on the lust for macho men, and mostly male audiences seem to be gleefully lapping it all up.

Not only do these movies almost completely lack any female heroes for us to cheer for, but the type of men being represented is not one that it's possible to emulate. These movies promote the celebration of violently dominant and emotionally stunted men. And there's not a single ounce of body fat on any of them.

Anecdotal evidence all but proves that, for decades, Hollywood had a real problem with the way it spoke to women about their weight. Casting directors would be so ruthless that even huge stars like Jennifer Lawrence admitted to being told she wasn't skinny enough, and was threatened with being sacked from a film if she didn't shed some weight. While I don't doubt it will have been happening for years, it's only recently that male actors have begun to speak out about this, too.

Take Chris Pratt as a perfect example. He was once labelled the 'sexiest man in the world', but even he suffered the humiliation of being fat-shamed by one Hollywood director who didn't think Pratt could hear him. The story goes that when he arrived for the casting session for *Guardians of the Galaxy*, Jim Gunn was reportedly overheard saying: 'Who do we have next? Chris Pratt? What the fuck? I said we weren't going to audition the chubby guy from *Parks and Recreation*.'

Despite his impressive career, Pratt had already been discounted from the role because he was apparently too fat. If you actually look at Pratt's character in *Parks and Recreation*, Andy Dwyer is a perfectly normal-looking guy. In reality, what this means is that while playing the part of an average man, Pratt wasn't walking around with a dangerously low body-fat percentage and wasn't hiring personal trainers to make him look like Michelangelo's David.

Now, I'm fully aware that *Guardians of the Galaxy* is about superheroes, and that superheroes are, by definition, meant to be superior beings. For the leading role I'm sure they were looking for something specific, but these are fictional characters. Actors should attempt to look a certain way for specific roles within reason, but directors need to take more responsibility for the mental and physical wellbeing of those they hire. Back in 1996, Matt Damon complained of suffering spells of dizziness when shooting *Courage on Fire* after losing too much weight too quickly. The world's best male athletes have body fat ranging from 6 to 13 per cent, and yet we regularly watch actors with levels as low as 4 or 5 per cent. By expecting actors to maintain impossible standards of body perfection at all times, the message is clear to those of us trying to live our lives outside the realm of fantasy: the only acceptable physique is a perfect one.

Bobby Holland Hanton, who was Chris Hemsworth's body double in *Thor*, has previously described how difficult it was to maintain his diet while training for the role. If you want proof that messages about how our bodies should look is being gobbled up by us mere mortals, *Muscle & Fitness* magazine even pointed out that 'Chris Hemsworth workout' was, at one time, the top search suggestion when you googled the actor's name. Similarly, if you type in 'Chris Pratt Guardians', then a suggestion suffixed with 'diet' will also come up – with a plethora of advice articles.

So, a male director told a male actor he was too fat, a body double found it difficult to maintain the perfect physique required of him, and yet men across the world are googling ways to try and imitate the whole stupid thing. The online bastion of laddishness the Lad Bible also gleefully body shames both men and women who dare to allow themselves to put weight on. In 2016 the site posted two pictures of *Prison Break* actor Wentworth Miller, one as his emaciated character, and one in real life with the caption: 'When you break out of prison and find out about McDonald's monopoly.'

It turned out that the photo of Wentworth they used was from 2010 and was taken during a time he was suffering from depression and suicidal thoughts. He responded to Lad Bible telling them 'I've struggled with depression since childhood. It's a battle that's cost me time, opportunities, relationships, and a thousand sleepless nights. In 2010, at the lowest point in my adult life, I was looking everywhere for relief/comfort/ distraction. And I turned to food.'

The website retracted their meme, and ran an apology promising they would 'continue to cover how prevalent mental health issues are among our audience, as well as the damaging stigma that surrounds such matters', but the disregard the site has for another human being is damaging – and points again to that much wider issue of men suffering from a lack of empathy.

What Wentworth's response and the Lad Bible's retraction showed is the power of challenging these behaviours. It's only by intervention that hurtful, negative actions will reduce in their frequency.

• • •

For decades women have increasingly expressed their dissatisfaction at how they are portrayed across the entirety of the media. Among the barrage of messages aimed at women, they've been told how to act, what to wear and how skinny they should be. Each of these ideals is a barometer against which a woman's femininity can be judged. Mountains of research over the years has proven that there has been a drastic effect on women's sense of self-worth and, despite the evidence clearly showing a link between the two, those calling the shots in the media sphere have shown little interest in changing their ways.

You only have to go to the *Daily Mail*'s website (the most visited English language news site in the world) to witness the shameful sexualisation and demonisation of women. It features a column on the right-hand side of the site, now commonly known as the 'sidebar of shame', which is adorned with hundreds of photos of women's bodies and describes them in a whole host of judgemental ways. It doesn't end with celebrities either. Think about how the media went ballistic over Theresa May wearing a pair of £1,000 trousers while pursuing an austerity agenda. She was lambasted for being 'out of touch' with the common voter, but during the entire premierships of her numerous male predecessors, nobody ever bothered asking how much their tailored suits had cost. Rhiannon Lucy Coslett grew tired of the way women were being portrayed in newspapers and magazines in particular and co-wrote a book called *The Vagenda: a Zero Tolerance Guide to the Media*, which focused on how women have been manipulated in the media for too long.

As she explained to me:

> if you want to sell more makeup and beauty products, you
> have to create a need in women to use those products. The
> simplest way to do that is to create an insecurity. Once that
> insecurity is created then you can come along like a fairy
> godmother and say 'here are all the things that can fix you,
> here are all the things that can make you a better human'.

She also thinks we've reached 'peak manipulation for women'
when it comes to advertising and shaming them: 'They're
running out of opportunities and women are beginning to
build up a tolerance to it, so they've started marketing towards men.'

She's right, too. It's no longer just women being targeted
by scurrilous advertisers and their money-driven campaigns
to coerce us into wanting to 'better ourselves'. It actually
began in earnest about ten years ago when advertisers finally
realised they'd been missing a huge marketing opportunity.
They'd become masters at warping the minds of women, so
it didn't take long for them to get into their stride when it
came to men.

Over time, all those same issues women developed began
to show up in men, too. In the three years I've been living
in London, there have been two unforgettable examples of
advertising showing complete disregard for those people
struggling with their body image or for those teetering on
the edge of serious psychological problems.

The first one smacked me in the face on the very first day I arrived, and was an advert for Marks & Spencer underwear. I'm fully aware that advertising boxers and briefs is going to require some flesh being shown, as only Superman wears his underpants outside his trousers. The model they chose to advertise middle-of-the-range underpants was David Gandy, and they plastered him over almost every wall of Oxford Circus tube station and beyond. Every morning, 100 David Gandys and their impossible abs all stared back at me and my fellow commuters. There was no escape.

For the first few days I wasn't even sure what product he was meant to be selling. All I could do was stare at muscles I didn't even know existed, or stare down at the floor so as not to let his smug face catch my gaze. The essence of the advert, and the reason companies like to use beautiful people on their ads, is to persuade you that if you buy the same underwear as David Gandy, you're going to look like David Gandy. Obviously that's nonsense, and the sad truth is that none of us regular folk will ever look like that – not least because it isn't possible to airbrush an already-phenomenal physique onto ourselves in real life. I'm sure their ad campaign was a success, but I haven't been into M&S to buy underpants, so it didn't have its desired effect on me. The effect it did have, however, was to shame me into thinking my flabby body was just not good enough – and I'm sure I wasn't the only one.

The second example of this sort of marketing caused such a huge uproar that protests saw Transport for London remove it from the tubes, buses and advertising boards all over the commuter network.

The offending advert was from the brand Protein World, and featured a woman in a bikini next to the words 'Are you beach body ready?' By chance, I'm sure, the model they chose happened to be bordering on malnourishment – you could see her ribcage sticking out below her not-well-covered breasts. The product they were selling? Their 'weight-loss collection'.

Protein World's owner is, predictably, a man. The head of marketing and head of products are both men, too. So that's three men in charge, who now brag about how much the furore increased sales, all the while acting with impunity and a total lack of empathy toward those suffering with body image problems for their own reward. And that's the problem here. There are massive rewards available for those willing to play on the insecurities of their target market. But, as Rhiannon rightly pointed out, the market for women may be saturated and, as proved by the protests against the ad, women are starting to fight back.

Men, however, aren't. And while the problems associated with body image in women are well-documented, there has only recently been a realisation that men are also being damaged psychologically by the images that surround us. Eating disorders have traditionally been seen as the preserve of women and young girls, but there's been a near 30 per cent rise in men suffering from a range of eating-related issues since 2000. It's now thought men now make up 15 per cent of those suffering from eating disorders in the UK, and that number looks set to continue to rise.

Dr Raymond Lemberg is clinical psychologist and an expert on male eating disorders. He says 'if you look at the Miss America pageant winners or the Playboy centrefolds or the runway models over the years, there's been more and more focus on thinness'. The playing field has levelled in the last fifteen years though, as movies and magazines increasingly display bare-chested men with impossibly chiselled physiques and six-pack abs. 'The media has become more of an equal opportunity discriminator,' says Lemberg, 'and men's bodies aren't good enough anymore either.'

This is something Sam Thomas agrees with. Sam told me he'd struggled to fit in at school. He says he was bullied badly between the ages of eleven and sixteen at his Liverpool secondary school because he 'wasn't a typical male' (watch out for David Gandy using this terminology to describe non-masculine men later in this chapter).

'I wasn't really that in to sports, or cars or even girls … and it was mostly homophobic bullying by other boys.' But Sam wasn't even aware of his sexuality at that time, and says the bullies only focused on him being gay because he wasn't trying to be masculine like his peers.

He began escaping from the bullying by hiding in the bathroom and would comfort eat, just as Wentworth Miller confessed to doing. Over time, he says, the binge eating, combined with anxiety and stress, meant he started making himself vomit. Having never been taught about mental illness and with no information available on the topic of men's mental health, Sam was in the dark. Even his doctor, while recognising Sam was suffering from depression, completely ignored his bulimia. According to Sam, 'people weren't prepared to accept men could have eating disorders' and it wasn't until he happened to pick up one of his mum's magazines that Sam realised bulimia existed, and that he was clearly unwell.

After leaving Liverpool and moving to Brighton, Sam says his whole outlook on life changed. He not only left his old life behind, but he also shrugged off the culture of masculinity he felt shrouded by at school. His bulimia began to fade and he found new purpose working with mental health charities, even spurring himself on to set up his own.

Sam founded the charity Men Get Eating Disorders Too, and now regularly speaks to a wide spectrum of people. He says the young people of today are facing problems schools 'just aren't equipped to deal with' and is adamant that it's of utmost importance young people are taught to understand how their minds are being manipulated and to spot the signs of problems arising.

His workshops identify the changing perception of the male body ideal and he told me he regularly asks those in attendance 'if they think body image ideals have changed in men in the last ten years' and says nearly everyone agrees that it has. He rightly points out that more cosmetics are now targeted towards men, and warns of the added peril of social media. He says 'all these indicators suggest that the pressure on men is more increased than ever before'.

Again, though, there's an odd paradox at play when it comes to how men view their bodies. The sight of ripped, toned masculine figures being trumpeted by the media not only leads to men wanting to shed weight in an unhealthy way, but it's also leading to some pumping their bodies with dangerous drugs as they attempt to rapidly grow their muscles or shed their body fat.

Lewis Brown was twenty-five years old when he decided he 'wanted to be better than anyone else' and embarked on a strict regimen of steroids and fat stripper pills. One day, he decided to take eight pills and ended up almost dying. It was only thanks to the quick-thinking of doctors who induced a coma and packed ice around his body that Lewis survived.

Ruthless money-makers are marketing products at people like Lewis knowing full well that enough young people are desperate enough to do anything to obtain the perfect figure and to spend all their money on their products. These things are just a click away. Hell, even some 'health shops' sell equivalents.

For a while I was that fat kid who was desperate to be slim, and so I immediately empathise with people who are badly affected by the imagery they see day-in, day-out. Remember I said I was so fat when I got home from university that I was barely recognisable? I'd managed to balloon to nineteen stone. Over the next few years I worked hard to bring my weight down in what I thought was a healthy and controlled manner. What I was actually doing, however, was resorting to drastic measures. My will-power was woeful and, despite exercising regularly, my lifestyle remained unhealthy. So, in the end, I started buying slimming aids.

When I lost some weight I was delighted, but never quite delighted enough. In fact I was never – and to certain extent never will be – completely satisfied. So, then I bought some 'fat strippers' and every day I put my body through the ringer. I took a dangerous amount of caffeine, in tablet form, along with other equally inadvisable things three times a day.

It was only when I forgot to take my pills that I realised how much havoc they'd been wreaking on my body. I had full-on withdrawals. Luckily I managed to recognise the problem in time and threw the remainder of my stash in the bin. Fortunately, over time, I came to accept that being healthy was more important than having a perfect physique. Health isn't necessarily what you see on the outside, and, once I realised that, my life was so much easier. But society continues to tell us the opposite.

While the true figure may never be known (as products are illegal and users are often reluctant to admit taking them), it's estimated that there's been a nearly 600 per cent increase in steroid use in some parts of the UK over the past ten years. Public Health England agrees that the true scale of steroid use is unknown, but figures suggest as many as 70 per cent of the users of state-funded needle exchanges (set up to help heroin-users access clean needles) are now used by those injecting steroids or growth hormones.

Jim McVeigh runs the Centre of Public Health at John

Moores University and is an authority on steroid use in the UK. He says that not only are users showing similar rates of HIV infection as heroin addicts, but 'the users of these drugs are taking higher dosages, using for longer periods and in larger combinations'. He also warns that the vast majority of products are manufactured illicitly, 'with no guarantee as to their contents or levels of contamination'.

In the legal market, the use of protein-based supplements has rocketed over recent years, as companies continue to toy with our body image anxieties. The real turning point for men was in 2005 when the body building behemoth Maxi Muscle decided to go mainstream and began advertising in lifestyle magazines rather than just targeting the body building world. They replaced the traditional Arnold Schwarzenegger physiques with what they'd like us to believe are more achievable athletic builds.

Their sales exploded almost overnight. As with all things successfully marketable, it didn't take long for other brands to follow suit. Men were hooked, and gyms across the Western world quickly filled with those wanting to achieve perfect abs. The campaign was so successful that, between 2007 and 2012, world sales in the protein industry doubled, and it's now estimated to be worth £8bn globally.

Noticing this trend in the media, the consumer analyst Mintel set out to discover just how influential advertising can be on men. In early 2016 they reported that men are becoming increasingly image obsessed and almost half of sixteen-year-old boys prioritised being in good shape over being in a relationship. Surely the reason behind them getting in shape is so they can attract a mate? Anyway…

Jack Puckett is a consumer lifestyles analyst at Mintel and said that 'The trend for using hyper-athletic male models and celebrities in advertising has grown significantly in recent years and has resulted in men today being just as sexualised in advertising campaigns as women.'

While these muscular role models create a level of aspiration for some men, for many more it has resulted in feelings of inadequacy – and, as Rhiannon explained, with inadequacy comes increased marketing opportunities. Whether through dangerous steroid use or an unparalleled thirst for protein drinks, men are becoming increasingly desperate to grow their muscles like never before. In the gyms across the country, men are now spending an inordinate amount of time, money and effort in sculpting what they believe to be the perfect body. But, as with all quests for perfection, the reality is never quite good enough and that's having huge mental health problems for the men caught up in the chase.

Dr Rob Wilson is a consultant psychiatrist and also the chair of the Body Dysmorphic Disorder Foundation, the world's first charity exclusively devoted to BDD. He agrees that men are increasingly feeling the pressure to look a certain way in order to appear powerful, successful and attractive. 'Muscle dysmorphia is a preoccupation with the idea that one isn't big enough, isn't muscular enough,' he explains. 'There are thousands upon thousands with it, who are going to be excessively concerned about their appearance, having very poor self-esteem, and also feeling very anxious and very worried.'

It's now thought as many as 10 per cent of the men you see using weights in your local gym suffer from this problem, but almost none of them have been diagnosed. Because society still promotes physical perfection and strength as a masculine goal, Rob says 'clinically speaking men aren't good at coming forward with this problem – they don't think it's psychiatric, they think it's physical'.

As a homogenous group, men choose not to recognise an obsession with muscle growth as being unhealthy. How many of us have seen these men in the gym and got a little jealous of their ripped muscles? We may not be addicted to growing our muscles, but we've definitely been conditioned to see muscular physiques as superior, and that can spur us on to go beyond reasonable methods to achieve the look we want.

From our Hollywood heroes to the average Joe in the gym, nobody is telling us that being healthy is what's really important. Instead, a huge number of men are desperately seeking perfection and, as Rob Wilson explains, 'individuals can become so ashamed of their bodies that they suffer serve emotional distress'. He told me that some men inevitably become so depressed and hopeless and that it can even lead to suicide. In fact, he says muscle dysmorphia produces the highest rate of suicide of any of the BDD related conditions.

When you think about how all-encompassing the lifestyle to attain serious muscles must be, it's not difficult to understand why. Rob says many of those he's come across in his work talk of 'spending hours in the gym and forgoing other things in their life'. He says they don't date and many have no interpersonal relationships whatsoever. In fact, the gym takes up all their spare waking hours and they have no other hobbies. Rob says 'that it all means their whole life flat lines' and even their careers begin to suffer.

• • •

Luckily enough, I was invited to attend the 2017 Advertising Week in London, where I took particular interest in one panel discussion entitled 'What Became Of The Likely Lads: How Marketing to Men has Evolved'. As you'd expect, the panel was extremely diverse, and made up of four middle-aged white men. By chance David Gandy happened to be one of them (introduced to a crowd of professionals as 'handsome, stylish and a magnet for women'), as were three blokes who've made their fortunes hawking products to the 'modern man'.

One phrase that kept being repeated over and over was 'status signalling'. These marketers recognised early on that men enjoy nothing more than being able to flaunt their success. One panellist, Robin Wright, is the president of Engine, a creative marketing business, and he told us that 'masculinity was once represented by the motor car, which was the ultimate status symbol'. He then explained how the issue for people like him was determining 'what replaces the car? Is it clothing, the restaurant visits ... we still have the same need even if a car doesn't deliver it. We need to show our status and if the car doesn't do it what does?'

Then came Gandy's turn, and he thought he had the answer. He explained, with no apology whatsoever, that he'd grown tired of the 'androgynous models' he'd seen being used by the big fashion houses and arrogantly described them as 'not attractive' and even describing himself as 'the classic good-looking guy'. Eurgh.

Continuing down this path, he explained that what he wanted to be was 'the representation of the masculine male, the James Bond', and rounded up his comments by describing many of his male model peers as 'not even male'. So, in Gandy's mind, it is the superior male physical form that is the ultimate status symbol. 'The ultimate alpha male look' is, apparently, the best way to prove your dominance. Excellent. We have the world's top male model telling men that physicality is of the utmost importance. And we wonder where men get their funny ideas from.

Initially I was delighted when, towards the end of the discussion, the topic turned to mental health. Not only did Robin Wright tell us that 'the last taboo in marketing is mental health and our industry is not doing enough in this area', he also recognised that if marketing businesses 'don't support the mental health of its workers, then it is letting them down'. Which is true, but while we can't ignore their workers, what about the people their marketing is ruthlessly targeting?

Then it was Gandy's turn again. He was all too familiar

with the shocking rates of mental health problems and suicide among men, but didn't notice his own rank hypocrisy when he said 'we stereotype men and put them in a box'. Right on, David, but it's people like you doing the stereotyping. It's you who, just twenty minutes previously, described androgynous models as 'not real men'. According to all four members of this superb cross section of society, 'real men' are underrepresented in the media and in marketing, and they all believe it's time manliness made a comeback.

What these advertisers have actually done is to help create a growing masculine anxiety, and it's quite obvious to spot its effects. Despite the panellists' comments, the ways in which a man can show off his masculinity go way beyond that of just appearing big and strong or being surrounded by women. As we've already discussed, 'manliness' is also about being able to prove you are a capable earner.

The adverts specifically targeting men in this capacity are almost on every other page of the likes of *GQ*, *Maxim* and other men's mags. Each one focuses on a different aspect of how a man can show he is a financial success. Ads flaunt £800 coats and £300 shoes. They show men in perfect suits leaning on perfect sports cars. And they show watches worth more than all of those things combined.

This isn't body shaming, it is lifestyle shaming – and it suggests you're just not good enough if you're not wearing this year's must-have 'time piece'. My £20 Casio is more than capable of telling the time, but that's not a marker of a real man, apparently.

I honestly can't think of anything more moronic than spending thousands of pounds on something with one basic function, and yet it's another one of those things men have been brainwashed to believe they should flash around to show off that they have money and, hence, some status.

When we're constantly attacking the minds of men in this way, and telling them how they should look, it's no wonder we feel it's perfectly acceptable to bully the fat kid at school, and helps explain why homophobia is still an issue. If you're fat or gay you're not exuding the stereotype of masculinity David Gandy and those who hire him would have you believe is superior. You're effeminate, or 'not a real man', apparently.

In order to fully understand how images and clever marketing can be damaging, it's necessary to look beyond the traditional media that has dominated for so long. When it comes to lifestyle shaming, you need look no further than social media.

While adverts and magazines were once the lion's share of our media diet, over the past decade the spotlight has broadened exponentially with the advent of the monumental game changers that are the likes of Facebook, Instagram and Twitter. Where once you needed fame, talent or an awful lot of money to gain a following, now, social media has opened up the entire world to the entire world, and the media landscape has changed forever.

What these new platforms allow us all to do is to share. We're now at the point where people have become so obsessed with their online presence that it's causing serious psychological problems. Research in to this area is still relatively new, as the technology itself has not been around for long, but there's a growing body of work and plenty of anecdotal evidence to suggest this should be a serious concern. According a report published by the Royal Society for Public Health, 'social media may be fuelling a mental health crisis' in young people.

The sole aim of these sites was, initially, to maintain friendships from afar and have the ability to share some photos, stories and events with them online. It's now evolved way beyond that, and has become an all-encompassing competition to try and show off your perfect life to acquaintances and complete strangers. Instagram, for example, is nothing more than a flurry of perfectly choreographed photos, staged specifically to try and gather as many 'likes' as possible. The thrill of gathering likes leads users to increasingly stylise their lives, and take selfie after selfie in the hunt for perfection.

Knowing full-well that 800 'friends' could see your entire life quickly led to an arms race of idealism. It didn't take long for us all to buy in to this notion, and utilise all available platforms to try and show off how great our lives are to a load of people who really shouldn't care. The likes of Instagram and Snapchat offer almost nothing but a medium through which we can photograph our lives and share them with the world.

As with the issues caused by advertising and the portrayal of men and women on our screens, you'd be correct in thinking young girls suffer most from the fallout of social media trends. Much like before, most of the early analysis was done to determine the detrimental effect these behaviours were having on young girls.

As the teenager June Eric Udorie wrote in 2015:

It's becoming more and more obvious how the pressures of social media disproportionately affect teenage girls. I can see it all around me. Pressure to be perfect. To look perfect, act perfect, have the perfect body, have the perfect group of friends, the perfect amount of likes on Instagram. Perfect, perfect, perfect. And if you don't meet these ridiculously high standards, then the self-loathing and bullying begins.

We already know that the pressure to cultivate a perfect image has had a lasting impact on the psyche of young women, but we're also lumping anxieties on to young men, despite already knowing what can happen as a result.

You may think women are more easily influenced by social media pressures, but a team of researchers from Lancaster University disproved that. They analysed more than thirty studies from around the world that focused on the links between social media use and mental health issues and made a quite astonishing discovery. They found that 'men may be more likely to engage in the social comparisons that lead to depression than women'.

This follows on from the idea that women are beginning to build up some form of immunity. Having been targeted with daily body shaming for so long, perhaps more women are becoming impervious to the potential pitfalls social media offers. Men, on the other hand, are seemingly increasingly likely to be caught up in the dangerous comparison games social media can offer, and it's starting to show.

Most of the top Instagram accounts are female film or music stars. The odd male footballers are popular, too, but there's one guy who has cultivated his macho image to perfection, and has gained 21 million followers as a result. His name is Dan Bilzerian and he epitomises all that is wrong with the social media world.

A professional poker player who was left a whopping trust fund by his father (a convicted fraudster exiled in the West Indies), Bilzerian uses his millions to fund an extraordinarily lavish lifestyle. A quick scroll through his photos and you quickly notice a theme. His entire life, according to Instagram, is spent in the company of barely dressed women, on his private jet, in ridiculous cars, surrounded by guns, or all of the above. Bilzerian adorns these photos with captions such as 'if you're thinking about getting married, just remember, one vagina for the rest of your life ... not smart'. Oh, and he is, of course, muscly beyond the realms of being healthy.

To his followers he is the 'King of Instagram', and it's not difficult to understand why so many young men idolise him. He plays up to all of the possible masculine tropes and serves to prize open the masculine anxieties of many young men around the world. To them he is a demigod living the perfect male life.

Bilzerian's situation being so uncommon helps explain why so many men are enraptured by his life. He openly admits to being morally repugnant – acknowledging that it stops him gaining endorsements – but he doesn't need the money; he already has it all.

He's acting with the utter impunity he feels his masculinity entitles him to. So much so, on International Women's Day he published a photo of him eating food from a plate placed on a topless woman's back. He captioned it: 'they are good for so many things'.

Remember, it's now thought men are the biggest culprits of social media comparisons. As we try and choreograph our own online presence, other men see the likes and followers they can gain and want in on the action.

So, while we may not upload anything like Bilzerian does, we try and show off the very best of our lives to the world. We talk endlessly about our gym routine or how many times we've been to Crossfit. We take photos of ourselves opening bottles of champagne with sparklers in the ice bucket. We upload pictures of ourselves with attractive women. We tweet about a pay rise or the latest car we've bought. In the end it's all an unfulfilling contest, but that doesn't stop us wanting the gratification on offer for each and every 'like' we get from our peers. We're all responsible for each other.

Scientists studying the social media phenomenon now believe our brains are becoming wired to social media gratification in the same way they become wired to the gratification of hard drugs. Do a line of cocaine and you get a rush of dopamine through your brain. Get fifty likes on Instagram and a similar thing happens.

A close friend of mine once admitted that if he uploaded anything to Instagram and it didn't get ten likes within ten minutes, he would always delete. When I asked him why, he said it's 'so when people scroll through my profile, they can only see pictures with lots of likes'. To him, and many like him, it's of utmost importance that his social media image remains blemish free. Clearly there's a strange embarrassment in posting a picture that doesn't gain 'enough' likes.

That's obviously a low level of social media anxiety, but it's not surprising that these negative behavioural patterns have become both increasingly common and severe. What's more, the advent of smart phones and a continually connected society means 6–16-year-olds are now spending almost double the amount of time in front of a screen every day than they did in 1995. The increase, from 3.5 hours to 6.5 hours, is extremely significant and helps to explain why so many more young people are developing a whole host of psychological problems.

Natasha Devon was the government's mental health tsar and runs an organisation called the Self-Esteem Team. She goes into schools to discuss body image and mental health with young boys and girls, and told me how the young boys she speaks to 'don't want to believe that they're vulnerable'. Clearly, the fact that we teach young boys to be tough and strong doesn't allow them to acknowledge their vulnerability to media influences – but the facts just don't lie.

Our collective egos are being challenged by the men able to flaunt their success all over our various screens and, rather than ignore the ludicrousness portrayed across social media, we're becoming increasingly determined to follow suit.

Recognising the power social media has over our minds, it wasn't long before the ad companies came strolling into that world. Brands now pay vast sums of money to those able to cultivate followers across their many social media streams, and that's only intensified the arms race towards perfection.

Natasha says the advent of advertising on social media has meant that our profiles are no longer just places to share. Instead, she says, it has 'blurred the lines between impartiality and advertising'. Whether we're a travel blogger, a physical trainer or a guy writing a book about masculinity, we're all now trying to sell ourselves and gather a bigger online audience.

In order to do that we, too, have to try and come across as the perfect form of whatever self we are trying to sell. In the process, many of us are losing our authenticity and with it we lose any sense of our true identity. That determination to constantly be on social media can become all-encompassing. Seventeen-year-old Danny Bowman admitted spending up to ten hours a day taking up to 200 selfies – none of which he deemed good enough to share online. His obsession took over his life to the extent he dropped out of school, crash dieted to try and improve his appearance and ended up trying to kill himself when he couldn't satisfy his own image-related desires.

Danny said one of the biggest issues he faced was the total inability to feel confident talking about his problems. It's an extreme case, but research has shown that, as with many of their issues, young boys don't feel comfortable talking about their newly developing body image problems.

The advertising think tank Credos was set up to highlight the responsibility brands have for their consumers. Their research shows that boys are becoming increasingly worried about their appearance. About half feel eating disorders and extreme exercising are now gender neutral issues, so it's not difficult to see where problems can arise. While the pathways might exist for young girls to discuss their problems, Credos's director Karen Fraser says 'the relatively low awareness of boys' body image issues among parents and teachers, coupled with a culture of boys not discussing their worries, makes it a tough environment for boys to seek support'.

With so much focus rightly having been put on the portrayal of women, there has been very little from men trying to protect other men. While we've all started discussing our appearance far more often than previous generations, our conversations about ourselves haven't been healthy, if they've happened at all. The media, in its many guises, has now become expert at regurgitating the harmful masculine stereotypes: and we're seemingly all too happy to allow it.

CHAPTER TEN

BACKLASH TO FEMINISM

'If you're accustomed to privilege, equality feels like oppression.' For the life of me, I can't find out who first uttered those words, but they are absolutely bang on the money when it comes to describing many men's attitude towards equal rights.

This similarly appalling quote also floats around: 'There is no male privilege … and feminists are a big part of the problem for why things are so bad for men and boys.' This time, I know precisely to whom to attribute that quote. Remember the name Mike Buchanan, who I'll come back to later in this chapter.

The women's equality movement has gone through many stages. From the suffragettes of the early 1900s, so desperate to vote that they hurled themselves under race horses, to the women's liberation movement of the 1960s and 1970s, who rallied against the rigidity of the social roles they were expected to fulfil, women have fought for gender parity throughout all our living memory.

Their grievances may have shifted over time, but as each new generation of women picked up the mantle, there has been an order of men steadfastly battling to maintain the status quo. I'm not here to give you a history lesson, but with each wave came fresh demands, as women began to recognise the injustices meted out to them by the patriarchal societies they live in.

Eradicating injustices, such as the fact that, up until 1991, the British courts deemed that a woman permanently signs over her body to a man as soon as she marries him, has taken centuries to achieve. The principle, established by Chief Justice Hale in 1736, had taken over 250 years to retract. In his *History of the Pleas of the Crown*, Hale wrote: 'The husband cannot be guilty of Rape committed by himself upon his lawful wife, for by their mutual matrimonial consent and contract the wife hath given herself up in this kind unto her husband which she cannot retract.'

To all those men who say that feminism is irrelevant and something to be pushed back, I say just LOOK at the battles generations of women have had to fight. LOOK at these monstrous legal rules that demeaned them for so long. Given how despicable laws like this are, it's hardly surprising women continue to fight so stridently to win their rightful place as men's equals in society.

From the earliest days of feminism as we know it, each fresh demand for equality brought responses from men concerned that women were trying to undermine the social order. Take this quote from Octavius Beale's book, written in 1911, *Racial Decay*:

> Unreasonable demands for exaggerated 'rights' of women will always find a limit in the fact that the majority of men will constantly prefer for wives those who do not claim such rights, but who rather seek their happiness in cultivating and developing their specially feminine virtues and attributes, apart from any aim at equality with men.

More than 100 years ago, men were already concerned about women wanting rights and were fearful of, as Beale put it, men being 'degenerated'.

British society was more than happy for women to 'do their bit' during the war, encouraging them to take up work in munitions factories as their husbands and sons were off fighting in Europe, but, once the war ended, the propaganda shifted and women were expected to get back in the home. And it's here some men wish they'd stayed.

Rather than just ignoring many of the problems men are responsible for, some men are utterly determined to try and prevent the quest for gender equality. Some go as far as blaming women for the injustices they perceive are meted out on men, and they call themselves Men's Rights Advocates (MRAs).

Since its inception in the 1970s, the men's rights movement has developed over time. It started off as an offshoot of women's liberation, with the men involved beginning to reject feminist principles. They felt women were focusing too heavily on themselves and trying to gain freedoms to the detriment of men. Feeling discriminated against, the men's movement began to try and push back against the tide of progression. At the very root of the men's rights movement is a sense of a loss of identity. They feel their masculinity has been challenged by a drive towards a more equal society to such an extent they feel their very existence has been cast in to doubt.

One of the earliest MRAs was Warren Farrell, and he campaigned to recoup some of the gender dominance he felt feminists had taken from men, particularly in the home, in schools and in the workplace. Men like Farrell completely rejected the move towards a more fair society, and instead suggested that women were trying to feminise their male environments and believed that was an inherently bad thing.

There was very little obvious growth in the movement over the past few decades, but more recently there's been a massive upsurge in the prominence of people describing themselves as MRAs and, while still a relatively small group, the movement has found a new voice via the internet.

The sociologist Michael Flood has studied the MRA phenomenon and told me it represents a 'more focused expression of a widespread discomfort, resistance and hostility among young men to the shifts in gender roles that the women's movement and feminism have brought about'. He says the men in these various different MRA groups 'are typically in their forties and fifties, often divorced or separated, and nearly always heterosexual'.

David Futrelle is a journalist in America and he's one of very few people with the patience to track the MRA movement. It's something he's managed to keep up with for years. He runs a website called We Hunted the Mammoth that focuses on, as he superbly puts it, 'an angry antifeminist backlash that has emerged like a boil on the ass of the internet over the last decade'.

David pinpoints the recent rise in popularity of the more virulent men's rights discourse that emerges online to 'Gamergate'. This was the 2014 scandal that surrounded female video game developer Zoe Quinn, who created a game based on her experience of depression. For some reason, the male-dominated industry took a disliking to this, and soon sites like Twitter, Reddit and 4Chan were awash with rumours about Quinn's sex life, as well as her phone number and address. The professional gaming community mostly condemned the misogyny Quinn was attacked with, but the rank sexism it had unearthed online hasn't gone away since.

You only have to glance at the Twitter mentions of any prominent woman to find a barrage of rape and death threats. Politicians, musicians and just about anyone in the public eye aren't safe from the trolls. Things are now so bad some female MPs set up a campaign called Reclaim the Internet, the name of which can be linked to the feminist objective of reclaiming the night. It is a campaign designed to make online platforms a safer place for women to operate, away from the bile and vitriol served up with an increasing regularity.

You might say that men suffer abuse online, too, and of course they do; but research by *The Guardian* found that eight of the top ten most abused writers online are female. The recent case of Lily Allen is a prime example of the hideousness of internet trolling. When debating immigration on Twitter in early 2017, she ended up facing a barrage of hatred that focused on the stillbirth of her son in 2010. One troll tweeted: 'The baby knew you were going to be such a horrible mother so it decided to go out on its own term[s].'

While it isn't fair to say that the MRA movement is defined by this sort of online activity, it is true to say that their movement legitimises the hatred of women – particularly those who are successful and in the public eye.

One of the most famous MRAs and rape-myth spokespeople is the now-even-more-disgraced-than-ever Milo Yiannopoulos. He's is a key member of the Alt-Right/MRA conglomerate (something I will discuss shortly) who feels that feminism is, as he put it, 'aimed squarely at undermining masculinity'. For a long time he somehow managed to remain relevant, despite promoting a whole host of ideas that were unashamedly anti-women, anti-diversity and anti any sort of decency in any way – even stating regularly that rich white men should be allowed to control the world. He's a professional antagonist who, having already been banned from Twitter for encouraging his followers to direct abuse at one of the stars of the all-female *Ghostbusters* reboot, fell from what little grace he had left by suggesting thirteen-year-old boys having sex with older men is perfectly acceptable.

Among the many disturbing headlines of articles he published on Breitbart – the news site and mouthpiece of the Alt-Right movement – were '"Slut's Remorse" is Why Rape Suspects Should Be Anonymised' and 'Feminists & Progressives Attack College Football with More Dodgy Rape Statistics'. He's the sort of person who tries to convince men not to attend consent classes and promotes the notion that women mostly fabricate claims of sexual assault. He once even stated that women saying that they 'feel harassed' is 'effectively meaningless'. It's interesting that, while MRAs dismiss what they perceive to be the 'feminist myth' of rape culture, many of the most ardent internet trolls are MRAs who regularly use rape threats as a way of intimidating women.

I approached a huge number of MRAs to learn more about their perceived sense of injustice, but found it almost impossible to gain access to them. Only two responded to my frequent requests. One, who had initially agreed to an interview, pulled out after reading the blurb for my book and deciding that I had 'sold out to the feminist line'. His name is Herbert Purdy and he expressly forbade any use, or citation of his work, before adding: 'I simply will not be a party to anything that adds to the misery of men.'

He then proceeded to send a 1,200-word email attempting to undermine my ideas. Without so much as talking to me, however, he unwittingly answering all the questions I would have asked him anyway. He emphatically stated that he is 'opposed to all that feminism stands for, on the grounds that it is the most divisive and socially corrosive ideology we have ever encountered'. On his website he admits to being 'part of an emerging world-wide movement, generically called men's human rights advocacy' and describes feminism as 'the biggest threat to our stability and social cohesion since the Second World War'.

His book, *Their Angry Creed: The shocking history of feminism, and how it is destroying our way of life*, asserts that rape victims can't cry rape unless they try and fight back against their attacker; that men who flash their genitals at mature women shouldn't be punished; and that feminism is merely a synonym for lesbianism. He's another one of those MRAs who believes that there's a 'feminist rape culture lie' and rape statistics show no increase, nor prevalence of rape, despite the recorded number of prosecutions for sexual assault being at an all-time high in the UK, with 97 per cent of prosecutions brought against men. You can make your own mind up about all of that.

The other response I got came from a guy called Mike Buchanan, the one I quoted at the start of the chapter. After founding the Anti-Feminist League in 2010, Mike now commits much of his time to leading the political party Justice for Men & Boys. J4MB are resolutely anti-feminist: their website promotes articles such as those outlining 'thirteen reasons women lie about being raped' and they present a prize for 'whining feminist of the month'. In 2015 Mike left the

Conservative Party following David Cameron's support for all-female shortlists, and the party ran for three seats across the UK in the general election of the same year. Throughout the entirety of our conversation and for about an hour afterwards, I sat dumbfounded in near silence as I thought about all the different ways he blamed almost all of society's problems on the promotion of gender equality.

Like most MRAs, he believes that the world is now set up for the advantage of women. He told me men are now 'born worthless' and 'have to work hard to achieve anything'. To translate, this means he thinks that, by virtue of being born with a penis, he should be treated better than anyone who isn't.

The sociologist Michael Kimmel says it's a perceived threat to men's entitlement that spurs on the MRAs. 'Without confronting this sense of entitlement, we will never understand why so many men resist gender equality. It's because we grew up thinking this is a level playing field and any policy that tilts it a little bit, we think it is reverse discrimination against us.'

Kimmel believes that 'white men in Australia, North America and Europe are the beneficiaries of the single greatest affirmative action program in the history of the world. It is called the history of the world.' This is fairly obviously true, but Mike Buchanan disagrees. He thinks that 'women are born valuable' and that men 'have to pander to them and sacrifice themselves to have sex' – whatever that means. Having been accustomed to privilege, to Herbert, Mike and men like them, the advancement of gender equality now feels like oppression.

Mike suggested I watch a 2016 documentary called *The Red Pill* – something he thought would 'open my eyes' to what he extremely patronisingly told me 'takes years' to understand. The 'red pill' of which the film speaks, is a nod to the iconic scene in the film *The Matrix* wherein Neo is offered a blue pill which will return him to his normal life, or a red pill which will let him see 'how deep the rabbit hole goes'. It's the fear of what's down the rabbit hole that the MRAs hold as their mantra. They believe they have seen the truth, while the rest of us are living in la la land.

The film is presented by an American woman called Cassie Jaye. For nearly two hours, she speaks to some of the biggest names in the MRA community and invites them to discuss their motives for joining the movement.

One of the major contributors is Paul Elam, the founder of A Voice For Men, the biggest MRA website in the world. Not only is he regarded as the one of the statesmen of the movement, he's also widely regarded (outside the movement) as yet another rape apologist – he once even admitted that, were he to be on the jury of a rape trial, he would vote 'not guilty' despite any evidence to the contrary.

Men like Paul believe that they have uncovered a hidden truth about the realities of the world but, as one contributor to the website VillageVoice.com described the documentary: 'Jaye tumbles slowly down America's stupidest rabbit hole, discovering that Men's Rights Activists are actually just dudes who have been dicked over.'

There is a huge flaw with the film, being that at not one

point do we see her challenge these men on some of the vile comments they have made in the past. Instead, Jaye sits passively as these MRAs spout their misogynistic bile; and, no doubt, they took this as a sign that they had won her over. Brainwashing comes up a lot in MRA circles and in his email to me, Herbert Purdy explained that 'young men like you have had their brains reprogrammed by the feminist zealots. I mean, think for yourself, for goodness sake.'

What Cassie Jaye does, to anyone not blinkered by their determination to remain inside their MRA echo chamber, is unwittingly highlight not only how awful a journalist she is, but also that these men constantly glaze over a fundamental truth.

Yes, men have legitimate grievances. But feminism isn't to blame for a single one; it's other men we should be holding to account. Take, for example, one of the biggest issues MRAs have with society: their belief that men's lives are viewed as far more 'disposable' than those of women. As proof, they point to the fact that a huge proportion of those killed in conflicts and wars across the world are male. They highlight that, for centuries and still to this day, young men are conscripted in to many countries' armies, while young women are not. Numerous MRAs interviewed in *The Red Pill* cited this as proof that men aren't cared for by society and yet somehow completely failed to recognise who it is starting wars in the first place. You only need to look at the list of all those tried and found guilty of war crimes to notice something every single one of them have in common: their Y chromosome. It wasn't until 2012 that a woman was indicted for war crimes at The Hague, and she was the wife of the former President of the Cote D'Ivoire, a man charged with orchestrating a campaign of violence in an effort to remain in power after losing an election.

And it isn't as though women don't want to join the front-line. Women have fought hard for their place on the battlefield, but when change was announced in 2014 there was pushback from people like Colonel Richard Kemp, who said he thought an effective fighting unit was best when it was only a 'band of brothers'. Many argued that women aren't fit and strong enough to fight. And while that may be the case for some women, I'm not fit and strong enough to join the army either. So I don't join. The same goes for everyone now, regardless of their sex.

It was also suggested that men on the front line would somehow lose their focus if they had to work alongside a woman they found sexually attractive. This merely points to the lack of professionalism and respect these men have towards their colleagues (and would also serve as an argument for completely splitting up the sexes in any work environment). In fact, that disrespect was proven by the discovery in 2017 of a Facebook group of over 30,000 US Marines who were disseminating naked pictures of their female co-workers.

It was also mooted that male soldiers might be inclined to act irresponsibly in order to save a female soldier. The idea that women need to be saved by men has come from a backlog of centuries of male violence; if there were no violence, there would be no aggressors from which to save a woman. No domineering men means no damsels in distress.

Guess what else happens when we go to war? Women and children die, too. In the Second World War, about 50 per cent of deaths were civilians. But it's not just death, either. Rape is also a massive problem during conflicts. You don't get thousands of women with guns marauding through foreign lands killing the men and raping the women, do you?

One of the main threads of the MRA agenda is to espouse that somehow women themselves have been hoodwinked by feminism and that they actually have no interest in being independent from the whims of their husbands.

Mike Buchanan is adamant that 'women want to work less' and 'the narrative you're hearing in the media is bullshit … it's feminist propaganda'. He then went on to explain to me that the trials and tribulations of the grossly underfunded and understaffed NHS could be attributed to the poor work ethic of women. He believes there's 'no evidence globally that women are, as a class, becoming more work orientated' and pointed to the fact women are far less likely to work full-time throughout their lives.

Despite ignoring the giant maternity-leave-shaped elephant in the room, this man genuinely believes that women can't and don't want to work and would be far happier reverting to the days of the domestic housewife. Herbert agrees. 'Who cares?' he asks when discussing parental leave. 'Men neither want, nor are able to take such leave. Their role is to be providers and protectors – at least, it was before young men fell into the trap of believing this feminist canard.'

According to two of the most prominent British MRAs, women don't want to work and men don't want to help raise their own children. For them, the 1950s was a golden age. A man could head to his all-male work to perform his manly duty as provider while his wife stayed at home to cook and clean the house in preparation for his return. On arrival, it would be pipe in hand and slippers on. Then, until the law was changed as recently as 1991, it would be sex with the wife whether she wanted it or not. What a life for him. Only for him.

If you look beyond the British men's rights brigade to similar groups in other Western countries, there is a tangible, terrifying sense that these men are achieving their bid to undo the equality and justice women have achieved. As I'll outline in more detail shortly, there is an almost identical parallel between the MRA movement and the Alt-Right. Both are railing against what they believe to be an affront to their right to rule the world, whether that be based on sex, religion or skin colour. You need only look at two of the policies the Trump administration attempted to enact within his first two months of his Premiership for proof of the similarities.

One of his first acts was to sign an executive order banning international NGOs from offering information about abortions if they receive US funding. The Global Gag Rule was a literal lifesaver for many women, particularly in poorer countries like those in sub-Saharan Africa. A photo of the moment of signing of the order was tweeted by the President, and showed him flanked by a phalanx of other middle-aged white men, each one as unbothered as the other that desperate women will try and abort their children anyway and that unsafe abortions kill tens of thousands of women every year.

Then came Trump's promise to 'repeal and replace Obamacare'. While he failed to get the bill passed, it prompted another photo of a room full of men sitting around discussing how changes might affect pregnancy and maternity care provisions. One Republican Congressman even asked why men should have to pay for prenatal care. In his second attempt at getting this bill passed, Trump ruled that women who have been raped suffer from a 'pre-existing medical condition' and so have to pay higher insurance premiums for their healthcare.

As I say, it is impossible to look at the Alt-Right and not see a large crossover when it comes to MRAs. What's more, when you analyse some of the language espoused by the Alt-Right, you can clearly spot a backlash against what is perceived to be the feminisation of society, and of men in particular. The most commonly used insult used by the Alt-Right is to call someone a 'snowflake'. A snowflake is fragile, and can be easily damaged. The Alt-Right and now the MRAs use this term to describe someone they deem liberal and likely to rail against social injustices. Feminists are forefront in their crosshairs.

Take, for instance, the self-entitled 'suffragentlemen' and author of *Stand By Your Manhood*, Peter Lloyd who, in a Sky

News debate with the comedian Kate Smurthwaite, stated that 'sticks and stones will break my bones, but there's always something that will offend a feminist.' Peter, like many MRAs and members of the Alt-Right, took great pleasure in Kate's angry response and mocked the fact she had been 'triggered', as if reacting to misogyny is akin to having a mental health problem. For them, Kate's reaction was classic 'snowflake' behaviour. In layman's terms, she was insulted; but, to the MRAs, it was 'just banter'.

One of their biggest put downs is the description of a man as a 'beta' because, of course, they are all obsessed with being viewed as dominant 'alphas'. To them, the masculine construct is gospel, and only the exalted alpha male status is acceptable.

Another term they use to describe men is 'cuckold', which is often shortened to 'cuck'. A cuckold is a man whose wife has slept with another man, so the widespread use of 'cuck' is the MRAs' way of trying to assert their dominance over men who have somehow found themselves on the wrong side of marital infidelity. It alludes to the fact these men have some-how lost control of a woman he should be dominant over. The MRAs have a fascination with sexual dominance, in part because many of them have been spurned by the women in their lives.

Then, when somebody shows signs of being offend-ed, the Alt-Right will describe them as being 'butt hurt'. Translated, it means you have been anally penetrated, i.e. correlating homosexuality with being weak. It's again about sexual dominance. That's the thing with these sorts of men.

They're so obsessed with the idea of their dominance that, now it's being challenged, they have resorted to creating their own hideous terminology to reinforce the ideals they'd love to see put in action.

The impact of MRA beliefs spreads far and wide, and it's not just American politicians trying to fight back against equality. There's a contingent of small-minded British politicians doing all they can to try and stifle legislation that would benefit society as a whole.

The Conservative MP Philip Davies is a frightening example of the insidious nature of the MRAs' fight against female progression. He's an avid supporter of men's rights campaigns, has been a speaker at the Justice for Men & Boys' Party Conference, and is trumpeted by MRAs as their lone voice in mainstream British politics. Davies has used his position in the House of Commons to regularly subvert bills any sane person would gladly wave through. His chosen tactic is to filibuster, whereby he talks for so long – often about irrelevant minutiae relating to a bill – that there isn't any time left for the debate to conclude or for a vote to take place.

In 2015 he famously obstructed a bill that would have made carers exempt from paying exorbitant hospital car park charges. This was not only a direct attack on an already underfunded service, but, given most carers are female, it was also an attack on the livelihood of women. His reasoning against the legislation was that it would reduce hospital revenues and could push up parking charges for other people – men, perhaps?

In an attempt to further undermine the work of MPs to achieve a fairer and more equal society, the Conservative Party allowed Davies to run, unchallenged, for membership of the Women and Equalities Committee – something he says shouldn't exist in the first place. Now, I'm not one for shutting down a debate, and Davies should be allowed to have his say, but one of his first acts as a member was to try and remove the word 'women' from the committee's title.

Laura Bates is the founder of the Everyday Sexism campaign and, after Davies joined the committee, wrote:

> He has previously described feminists as 'zealots', voted against equalities legislation, argued against equality targets in the workplace and once tabled a private member's bill that would have repealed the Sexual Discrimination Act 2002 [...] like many misogynistic so-called 'men's rights activists', Davies does a disservice to genuine concerns about issues that have an impact on men.

Perhaps even more damningly, Davies also attempted to derail the ratification of the Istanbul Convention, an act that signifies the global effort to try and reduce levels of violence against women and girls. Rightly, Davies pointed out that men are often also on the receiving end of domestic violence, and continually referred to the fact the bill doesn't try and put in place any protections for men and boys. Davis also tried to talk down the proposed Crime Bill to end the use of the term 'honour killing' in relation to domestic violence and to enforce the prosecution of those who beat and murder British women abroad. In the Commons, he asked 'Why do we need to have just females mentioned in this bill? Why cannot it be for all victims of these terrible crimes?' This, despite the female MP who introduced the bill clearly stating that honour killing is 'a violent criminal act – sometimes committed against a man, but more often against a woman'. Despite speaking for ninety-one minutes, the bill passed by 138 votes to one. No prizes for guessing who the lone dissenter was.

While Davies is presumably acting upon a desire to protect men's rights, he is actually doing more to threaten rather than preserve them. It is an awful fact that men do suffer at the hands of abusive partners and men's rights activists are right when they say that there are so few male refuge centres. But, by cultivating a landscape wherein it is acceptable to use homophobic language as insults, these activists are merely propagating the difficulty many men have when it comes to admitting that they need help. Men are afraid to come forward because they face ridicule. And it's the MRAs who mete it out.

The sneering attitude of many MRAs only serves to alienate them from serious debate about issues that actually do warrant some focus. Philip Davies is in a privileged position of influence and could, in his own mind, actually be trying to help men by focusing on problems such as the lack of refuges available for male victims of abuse. However, his strategy of undermining the excellent work many women have achieved over years only serves to make life worse for women, rather than improving life for men.

This is the sorrowful case when it comes to many issues impacting men today. Mike Buchanan pointed out to me that 90 per cent of the UK's homeless population are men. While this is a shocking statistic that warrants a response, he, like almost all other MRAs, simply points out the problem and then doesn't actually do anything constructive to try to solve it.

Not only do MRAs blame women for male woes, but they try to co-opt women's rights activism for the advancement of their own agenda. Take, for example, the deserved media prominence given to the outrageous practice of female genital mutilation (FGM) over the last few years. MRAs wrongly conflate FGM with male circumcision, and the fact that FGM is designed to obliterate any chance of women enjoying sexual arousal whereas circumcision does nothing to prohibit men's sex lives is no matter to MRAs. It is interesting, though, that if you type 'end FGM' into Google you're hit with group after group, all of whom have active campaigns to stop this abhorrent violence against women; and yet, despite the MRAs' numerous protestations about it, googling 'end circumcision' results in a handful of patchy campaigns and only one of these is in the UK, whose website hasn't been updated since 2012. However, while I'd back any campaign to end the practice, circumcision should not be confused with FGM. MRAs simply see that women are receiving attention for a very real problem and try to hitch a ride on the back of women's activism.

While MRAs are correct to highlight issues facing men

today, what are they actually doing to try and combat these? And how are we supposed to give their arguments the time of day when they highlight legitimate issues and claim – as they did in the J4MB 2015 election manifesto – that 'women are arguably over-represented as MPs' in the same breath?

• • •

Leniency in sentencing is a huge focus of the MRA movement, and they regularly highlight cases of violent women escaping a custodial sentence. The criminal lawyer Joseph Kotrie-Monson explained to me that the reason violent men are given tougher sentences and longer stretches in jail is because it's widely accepted that 'if men spend long enough inside, the prison system neutralises their violence'. He says jail time 'breaks them' and 'has a dulling effect on their violent tendencies after three to four years'. This isn't the case for violent women, however, who are generally far less likely to reoffend if they receive a community order rather than jail time. Again though, rather than to try to reduce the number of incarcerated men, Philip Davies and other MRAs' illogical response is to campaign for more women to be sent to prison.

What they fail to recognise is that one of the other reasons women are also treated more leniently by the courts is that an estimated 17,240 children are separated from their primary carers due to imprisonment every year. Judges are far more reluctant to incarcerate somebody who is the sole carer of a child and, as we know, mothers account for about 90 per cent of single parent families.

One MRA agenda I have some sympathy with is the often quoted issue of a father's right to access their child following an acrimonious divorce. Women are far more likely to be given custody of their child and fathers are often forced by law to pay huge sums of money to their estranged spouse to help raise their child.

For men, the statistics are actually frightening. More than 90 per cent of child custody cases involve men trying to gain access to their children. While over three quarters of those cases will end with the father being granted some access, it is mostly limited to winning the right to have their child stay overnight or every other weekend. For some, access can be as limited as seeing their child during the day, whereas about 25 per cent will be given only supervised access or none whatsoever.

On the surface it could be seen that men are being treated unfairly, but given the way society is structured it can hardly be surprising that we aren't granted nearly the same privileges towards children as women. It isn't written anywhere in British law that mothers should be granted greater access to their children than fathers. It is merely down to each individual judge in each individual case, so why are men so infrequently chosen to be the primary care giver?

For centuries men have left the day-to-day child rearing to their wives – and that's merely being reflected in the courts. Things might be changing now, and more fathers might be choosing to engage with their children's upbringing than in previous generations, but societal structures still prevent too many men from balancing their careers with bringing up their children. There's still too much focus on a nuclear family where a man earns the money and a woman raises the children. We know that very few men feel able to take up shared parental leave, so it's fair to say that women are spending the most time with their children. It's therefore not difficult to understand why a court would deem a mother the more adept and suitable care giver than the father. And with so many fathers out earning the money, it's not surprising that they will be legally obliged to stump up the lion's share of the child maintenance funds.

Of course there are cases where wives can become too de-pendent on the finances of a wealthy ex-husband; but, where children are involved, a man who has gone out to work and left his wife to raise the children should not be shocked when he is expected to fork out some money to aid the child's upbringing.

Paul Elam is a divorcee who rails against the 'injustices' men face in family courts; only, what men like him rarely discuss is the reality of their own lives. He once wrote that 'fathers are forced to pay child support like it was mafia protection money', despite him having accused his wife of lying about being raped so he could avoid having to pay any child maintenance.

The MRAs are leading the call for us to return back to the days of 2.4 children and a household where the husband is the breadwinner and his wife cooks and cleans. But they are the same men who then lament the courts' decisions to grant custody to the mother.

They just don't see this quite obvious correlation.

Many of the MRAs are divorced husbands who seem to spend an inordinate amount of time trying to undermine their former spouse's ability to be a successful parent. In his book *Angry White Men* Michael Kimmel highlights the case of one child who told his custody evaluator his dad didn't spend a lot of time with him 'because he's always busy working on his fathers' organisation'.

Michael Flood recognises how counter-productive these movements are. He says 'some men go through traumatic experiences like a brutal separation and lose contact with their children'. Rather than receiving the support they need, these groups 'fix men in their victimhood. They blame the system, blame feminism or blame their "bitch of a wife"'. That all acts as a distraction from questions he could be asking himself about why his wife left him, or why he wasn't granted custody – which certainly doesn't help him to heal, nor does it improve his chances of being more involved with his children in the future.

Research in the US shows that 91 per cent of couples come to their own custody arrangement without the help of the court system, and, of those, the majority of these couples agree that the wife should be the primary carer. What's more, only 4 per cent of custody disagreements end up being decided by a family court. That means in America (where the MRA movement is most widespread), most men actually choose to give the mother custody of their children. If so many men relinquish primary carer status of their own volition, it's not surprising the courts reflect that trend.

For those who are denied the access they'd like to their children, men as a whole have to take some responsibility. Of course there will be individual cases of vindictive mothers making false accusations of neglect or violence, but the masculine construct of family life has led to too many men becoming estranged from their children both before and after divorce.

• • •

There's another thing the MRAs are determined to blame on women, and that's violence. Many of them are utterly convinced that mothers are to blame for their violent sons and husbands. The first time I heard this idea I had no idea how widespread that belief is, and only found it out while doing an interview for a radio show in Los Angeles hosted by a man called Jesse Lee Peterson. He runs the organisation 'BOND', dedicated to 'Rebuilding the Family by Rebuilding the Man', and in our chat about how men become violent he told me that 'the anger you see inside of a man is that of his mother'. Chin on floor.

He went on to explain his belief that it's 'unnatural for a man to be a violent person' but says the 'lack of patience and the yelling' they receive makes them 'resent their mother' and that explains why young men become violent. He attributed it in particular to the rise of the single mother and says it's why 'violence increased in the 1960s'.

In an article he wrote shortly after Elliot Rodger went on his killing spree, Peterson tried to blame Rodger's violence on the fact he was raised by his mother, before adding that 'what he needed most was the love of his father'. Quite right, too.

This is an argument Herbert Purdy made to me. When responding to a question about male violence I hadn't even had the chance to ask, he asked me if I'd 'stopped to ask who it is that has brought them up this way in our increasingly single-mother society?' Again, here's another MRA suggesting that male violence can be attributed to present mothers while conveniently ignoring the absent fathers. Purdy is adamant that 'the hand that rocks the cradle rules the world, after all'.

Much of the MRA agenda now goes a lot further than simply apportioning blame. One offshoot of the movement is a group called Men Going Their Own Way (MGTOW) that claims to have sworn off women for good. While the MRAs can at least claim to be involved in at least some fairly light activism, these guys certainly can't. Their entire raison d'être is to detach themselves from women altogether (something I'm sure many women are delighted about) and create an online 'manosphere' wherein they can air their combined grievances. Given they're supposed to have 'gone their own way', it's strange how much of their time is spent discussing women and sex.

David Futrelle told me that the big point of overlap for these groups is 'sexual fear and resentment', suggesting the thing that gets them both viscerally angry is sex. Some of these men seem to genuinely believe that the lack of sex they're getting is a violation of their human rights.

More worryingly, that obsession with sexual dominance

means the MGTOWs and the Alt-Right groups are now slowly converging. As the Alt-Righters become increasingly sexist, so the MGTOWs are becoming increasingly racist. Futrelle says 'the two movements are drawn together by a shared obsession with, and paranoia about, the sexuality of women'.

For the Alt-Right, there is a constant fear that white women are diluting the purity of the white race by sleeping with black men. They don't seem to mind when a white man is sleeping with a black woman, because that scenario doesn't threaten their sexual dominance. Andrew Anglin is the editor of the popular website Daily Stormer and wrote that he reacts with 'a lot of anger' when he sees a black man dating a white women 'because it's OUR WOMB – that's right, it doesn't belong to her, it belongs to the males in her society – that is being used to produce an enemy soldier'.

Meanwhile, David points out that the MGTOWs are similarly obsessed with women sleeping with all other men. He says that 'while MRA complaints often reek of sexual insecurity and aggrieved sexual entitlement, MGTOWs seem to be motivated by little other than their own sexual anxieties and resentments'.

These men have an unrelenting fascination with the idea that young, attractive women ride a so-called 'cock carousel' when they are in their early twenties only to settle down once they have 'hit the wall' and their beauty begins to wane. Their masculine insecurities kick in when they believe women recognise this, and then turn away from the alpha males and towards men like them.

Clearly, the MGTOWs have an absurd amount of sexual entitlement, and a community like the ones being created online allows them to openly discuss their issues. The biggest problem, however, is that, as we already know, with masculine anxiety comes violence.

James Jackson is a case in point. He recently killed a black man in New York in an attempt to try and scare white women away from dating other black men. Not only was Jackson a subscriber to neo-Nazi and extreme right-wing sites, he was also a member of numerous MGTOW sites, too.

Many of these young, white men will have been drawn to the Alt-Right after being brainwashed by a diatribe of hatred towards ethnic minorities, but when they arrive are also radicalised against women. The poisonous vitriol encouraged by the Alt-Right means that it's sadly unsurprising that men like Jackson feel compelled to carry out extreme acts of what they deem to be revenge against women, or the men they feel are a threat to their sexual dominance.

You may say that this is a mostly American issue and that the Alt-Right movement hasn't gained too much traction in the UK, but the internet has no borders. The fact we now have an MP happy to openly admit to being an MRA and the increase of the prominence of MRAs both online and offline mean we in the UK must be vigilant.

The entire MRA/MGTOW/Alt-Right agenda embodies the very essence of toxic masculinity. Its members feel their rightful place as the sexually dominant, breadwinning head of a household has been corrupted by women and people of ethnic minorities and their mutual struggle for equality. And they're absolutely right. White men are no longer entitled to all of those things, but their reaction is to fight back with misogyny, racism and hate, and thereby inadvertently further ostracising themselves from a world that will one day leave them behind. If we don't talk to young men and ensure that they understand equality is not a threat to their existence, it won't be long before we lose more of the young generation of men who are almost permanently glued to their computer screens and to this extremist fearmongering.

In fact, one of the UK's leading Alt-Righters is Paul Joseph Watson, the editor-at-large of the site Infowars. He's already boasted about the fact that while liberals are busy 'virtue signalling' on Twitter, he is 'red pilling an entire generation on YouTube'. We may laugh at him, but teenage boys don't watch Channel 4 News, nor do they listen to BBC Radio; some are getting their 'information' from people like Watson, Paul Elam or Mike Buchanan who are utilising the power of the internet to further their dangerous causes.

Younger generations use YouTube far more than any other medium, and many of Watson's videos demonising women (such as 'Hot Women in Ads Banned to Please Fat Feminists') have already had hundreds of thousands of views. There are clearly plenty of people out there watching them, so it's ignorant for us to suggest people like him aren't having an impact: and teenage boys are some of the most susceptible viewers of them all.

CHAPTER ELEVEN

IT'S TIME TO TALK

About a month ago I found myself alone in an east London pub, awaiting the arrival an old friend from Manchester. For my sins I'm still partial to the odd cigarette when I drink, but there's a bonus to being a social smoker these days, being that I often find myself enjoying them in the company of total strangers.

On this occasion a fairly elderly gentleman approached me and asked if he could 'borrow one'. I obliged and postured the usual small talk/pleasantries we all fall back on in those situations. Ordinarily in London, and despite my best efforts, those conversations end far too abruptly, but this one didn't and it's a good job, too.

The man's name was Alan and he's lived one hell of a life. Aside from a couple of unsuccessful years in the army, he'd been living in and around Hackney for all his sixty years; only now he has no place to live. You could tell he hadn't been out on the streets very long, but that wasn't to say he wasn't suffering. In fact, quite the opposite. So we take a seat, I leave my cigarette packet open, and we talk.

He starts off by telling me that he's been kicked out of his temporary accommodation because he got too drunk (it turns out he gets drunk every night) and ended up in a scuffle with another of the men there. This wasn't a first offence. He explains that this was a pattern he'd been repeating for too long, and not just in the shelter. When I casually asked him why, I received a stark lesson about what can happen if you bottle up your emotions.

When Alan was ten years old, he saw his older brother fall from an unsurvivable-height. His 'best mate I ever had' hit the ground and died in front of him. For more than fifty years Alan has been blaming himself – convinced that calling out to his brother contributed to him leaning too far over the railings. Not only that, for fifty years he's quite clearly been suffering from severe post traumatic stress disorder – something he only bothered to get diagnosed when a lawyer recently said it might keep him out prison.

He says he felt okay as a youngster. His father, though clearly affected by what happened, steadfastly refused to talk about the accident. In all his remaining years, Alan said he barely heard his dad mention his brother again. In fact, the only time he saw him cry was at the funeral, but only when he thought nobody could see him. Alan admits seeing his dad fight back his emotions taught him to do the same, and it's a fight he's attempted to keep up ever since.

As he entered his teens and then adulthood, Alan said he

found himself becoming more and more frustrated with life, and gradually became depressed, angry and violent. 'It's too late for me', he said, wiping beer out of his beard. 'I've closed myself off forever, and the only way I deal with it now is by drinking or lashing out.'

I ask who he lashes out at, and he talks at length about being kicked out of school, the army, numerous jobs, his first and, latterly, second marriage. All, he says, down to the violent tendencies brought on by his mental turmoil. 'Not just towards other people, either', he continues, almost smirking. He then stands up to take off his coat, rolls his shirt sleeves up and reveals an arm with more scars than a butcher's block. For good measure, he shows me the other – it's in no better state.

It's about that time my friend arrives. I've known Alex since we were eleven, but we naturally drifted apart as we've got older. Only there's something I found out about Alex much more recently than either of us had wished. I ask Alan to get his arms out again and, as he does, Alex rolls up his sleeves too. He simply says: 'Snap!'

Both these men go about their daily lives and, to look at, you'd have no idea what was lurking beneath the surface. But both of them talk a very similar game. Sure, Alan may have suffered horrible trauma, but the ensuing mental health problems were impossible for him to talk about. Likewise for Alex, who openly admits that the stigma of his bipolar has made it extremely difficult for him to open up about his difficulties, particularly to his male friends. Both have a predilection towards excessive alcohol use, both have done astonishing amounts of harm to their own bodies and, while only Alan has attempted suicide, both have contemplated it.

Before Alex and I left the pub that night, having spent so long in conversation we were horribly late for dinner, he and Alan took over the conversation. As they swapped stories and debated which of their antidepressants was best, I sat back, listened and was struck by their candour.

I know Alex, and he'll only usually talk to those closest around him with such openness, while Alan was a stranger, and had admitted from the start he's a closed book. But here we all were, talking, and I could clearly see the good it was doing both of them. It could easily have been the case that both these guys were no longer with us. The sad reality is that there are far too many men for whom that is a reality.

As we already know, men are killing themselves at an alarming rate, and when you break those statistics down, you understand that this is not simply because young men are otherwise healthy. The suicide rate is still rising, and something needs to be done. The harsh realities are that, of the 6,000-plus people killing themselves every year in Britain 75 per cent of those are men. For every female suicide, there are three men no longer with us.

The Office for National Statistics tells us that, over the past ten years, the male suicide rate has steadily increased, while for women, it has remained all-but the same. Why is this happening?

The NHS website tells us that 'in the UK, research has

shown us many people who die by suicide have a mental illness, most commonly depression'. So, it would make sense that, given men's propensity to take their own life, they have a far higher rate of depression and mental illness than women.

The Mental Health Foundation state that in England (granted not the entire UK, but let's not split hairs), 'women are more likely than men to have common mental health problems'. In fact, one Oxford University professor concluded that studies show women are 75 per cent more likely than men to have recently been diagnosed with depression.

How is it possible that more women suffer from depression, and yet men are killing themselves at a far more alarming rate? There has to be some explanation. Perhaps depression just hits men harder? Perhaps depression is like the flu; women may get depressed, but maybe men get man-pressed? Maybe women are genetically able to cope better with mental illness? The answer is fairly simple: women are better at seeking help.

That NHS website quote I gave you on what leads to suicide earlier was actually incomplete. It should have finished with '…or an alcohol problem'. This is the reality for men when it comes to dealing with their problems. As outlined by that same ONS survey I've already cited, rather than ask for help when we're struggling with something, we turn inwards and try to self-medicate. So much so, the number of men receiving treatment for alcoholism in this country is three times that of women. Fortunately there are some amazing men sharing their experiences with the world in the hope that others don't make the same mistakes.

A famous example is that of Jonny Benjamin. Things could have been very different for Jonny if it weren't for a stranger talking him down from a ledge in 2008. He now tours schools and businesses across the UK talking openly about his mental health problems, and has recently been awarded an MBE for his services to mental health. I met Jonny to talk about his life before and after that day, and was mesmerised by how open he was about everything.

Jonny says he was a sensitive boy who often cried. Throughout primary school he found himself being progressively ostracised from the activities his male friends were participating in, because he 'wasn't sporty and competitive'. Instead he focused on his studies, as it allowed him to hide himself away and therefore mask his issues.

As he got older he was regularly told that 'boys don't cry' or that 'crying is for girls' and so he increasingly forced himself to suppress his emotions, only crying when he was alone. This continued through secondary school where, again, he hid behind his good grades, and at a bigger school it was even easier for him to disappear.

The examples of masculinity he saw in the world around him meant he didn't feel able to open up about his feelings to anyone. It meant he maintained the facade of being okay, because he felt 'ashamed and embarrassed' to admit otherwise. 'Weakness isn't something men are supposed to show. I'd seen men cry at the football, but before and after the game these men were always trying to prove how tough and strong they were.'

It wasn't until he was seventeen that a friend dared to suggest something might not be 'okay', and that's when he first sought diagnosis for a multitude of psychological problems, ranging from schizophrenia to depression.

He was referred to a centre for young people concerned about their mental health, but the waiting list was months long, leading Jonny to believe his problems 'weren't particularly important'. But his delusions got so bad that, by the time he was twenty, he believed his life was being played out like *The Truman Show*; and one day, he decided enough was enough.

Fortunately for us all, at the moment Jonny was about to take his own life, a stranger walked past and convinced Jonny to climb back from the ledge. For years afterwards, he still felt unable to fully divulge the realities of his condition. It wasn't until a male family friend had a heart attack and opened up to Jonny about his emotional state that he found the strength to speak openly, not only about what had happened, but more importantly about how he was feeling. That night Jonny went home, turned on his camera and 'just started talking'. He says he felt an almost 'instant relief not to be burdened with all the thoughts and feelings' he'd had in his head for years.

After posting the videos to YouTube, responses from other young men and women telling him they've 'been through this, too' came pouring in. With each video, he says his shame and embarrassment ebbed away: 'all the paranoia and insecurities diminished. It's cathartic, and that's why I still do my talks.'

Jonny now goes in to schools and shares his past traumas and explains his path to recovery. He says his honesty means many of the pupils open up for the first time about their problems. He now recognises the conditions which meant that he felt forced to hide way his emotional suffering, and also recognises that young people now have even more pressure on them to appear 'okay'.

'Young people have huge concerns about their bodies, and about social media. I'm always learning from them', he says, 'and I get inspired as these kids start encouraging each other to be more open.'

Jonny may be exceptional, but his experiences certainly aren't the exception. He just happens to be living proof that the rigid prism through which we allow ourselves to view masculinity can have a drastic effect on the men it influences.

• • •

At the start of the book, I outlined the stark male suicide statistics in the UK. That fact was the catalyst for me to start writing in the first place. Having never suffered mental ill health, I wasn't aware of its devastating consequences, nor its true scale.

Before working in journalism, I'd been one of those obnoxious idiots who thought somebody with depression just needed to 'cheer up'. I didn't know anybody with a mental illness, or so I thought, so I didn't understand how much suffering it inflicts on people. It was only after speaking to people that I realised how terribly misguided I'd been.

In my defence, I'd never been taught about mental illness. In the same way nobody ever showed me how to use contraception, nobody had alerted to me the fact mental health problems were no less a disease you need treatment to recover from than malaria until I reached my mid-twenties.

By not properly teaching young people about mental health problems, we turn sufferers into the 'other'. This lack of widespread information has led to both ignorance and fear of speaking out. No wonder those stigmas mean men continue to hide and deny their problems. And hide them we certainly do – while one in four women will at some stage in their lives receive treatment for depression, just one in ten men will seek similar help.

Damien Ridge, a professor of health studies at the University of Westminster, says society thinks men are doing pretty OK compared to women, but 'that when men talk about depression on their own terms, quite a large proportion are not doing so well'. And, clearly, we're not.

The clinical psychologist Martin Seager told me that if we're to improve the outcomes for men with mental health problems, it's imperative that we tailor services to suit men's specific needs. He says 'we either say that all young men are emotionally illiterate, or we accept that mental health services are gender illiterate'. I'd argue both sides of the argument have some validity.

Firstly, I'd say far too many men are bordering on emotional illiteracy and don't have a healthy relationship with their feelings, and that's certainly been proven by many of the conversations I've had while writing this book. Many men of all ages have told me they've felt stunted by the pressure on them to remain 'strong' and maintain an air of invincibility. Many young men take the ultimate step because they've suffered an unwelcome change in their lives and don't have the coping mechanisms in place to recover.

Secondly, throughout this book, I've been advocating that it's time for us all to drop the gender tropes that I and many others believe are causing the majority of the problems men face today. And yet, while I do strongly believe that, I also agree with Martin's point about mental health services often being gender illiterate.

Given how adept we've all become at keeping the realities of our problems locked away, it should be no shock that little attention has been given to male mental health recovery over the years. It's hardly surprising that many mental health services aren't all that well equipped to deal with male minds.

Damien Ridge also agrees that some mental health professionals were unable 'to pick up or spot the coded ways that men talk about their distress'.

'It's well-known that men do things like self-medicate or become angry or become somebody else's problem when they're distressed,' he says. 'Men let it build up then they lash out at themselves and other people. There's even an idea that there's a male kind of depression.'

Most symptoms of male depression aren't too dissimilar to those of women. A sudden loss of interest in work or hobbies, weight and sleep disturbances, fatigue and concentration problems should all set off warning lights, but they aren't the most common. There is another category known as 'stealth symptoms' which are far more likely to present in men and are also more often overlooked. Male depression can manifest itself as something as common as backache, meaning the underlying condition doesn't get treated, as we might only seek remedy for the physical pain. Some men turn to violence as a means of trying to cure our emotional pain, while some men can become abusive as a way of trying to regain some control in their lives. Most common of all, though, is an increased recklessness, particularly when it comes to our use of substances – particularly alcohol.

Given how, as men, we're conditioned not to acknowledge our emotions, too many of us turn to alcohol as a means of suppressing the anguish we may have inside us – something I know only too well. That's probably why the NHS estimates nearly one in ten men in the UK have some form of alcohol dependency, more than double that of women. But, and as we probably already know, the Mental Health Foundation tells us that excessive drinking 'can make existing mental health problems worse'. Those who turn to alcohol when suffering from even the most minor mental health condition will only exacerbate their mental problems. In turn that is likely to increase their dependency on booze and the cycle becomes very difficult to escape from.

You may wonder why, if a man is becoming violent or drinking too much, we don't spot more quickly that something is amiss. If you think about the construct of masculinity, however, we've come to regard these as common male traits. Why would anyone consider a man to be abnormal or suffering a crisis when he's acting in ways men are culturally expected to? Fortunately, there are now numerous charities highlighting male mental health that are at the frontline of breaking down the stigma surrounding male emotions. One of the most successful of these campaigns is CALM, the Campaign Against Living Miserably. Not only do they offer support to men in crisis, they also work towards challenging a culture that prevents men seeking help when they need it. Their big focus is to restructure male beliefs and put in place a more tolerant version of masculinity. CALM say they 'believe that there is a cultural barrier preventing men from seeking help as they are expected to be in control at all times, and failure to be seen as such equates to weakness and a loss of masculinity'. One of their main focuses is to circulate the personal experiences not only of celebrities and those in the public eye, but also of 'real people' in their bid to normalise conversations about mental health. CALM believes that 'if men felt able to ask for and find help when they need it, then hundreds of male suicides could be prevented'.

Towards the end of 2016 they produced a 'masculinity audit' aimed at discovering the main issues men were affected by, and how few of us are seeking help. The research suggests that as many as 50 per cent of their respondents admitted having felt 'very depressed' at some stage of their life, but barely half of those had told anyone about it. Among men aged twenty-five to thirty-four, the number of men feeling 'very depressed' rises to two thirds, with the main reasons listed as mental health, financial problems and relationship breakdowns. CALM say that 'while men were less likely to have been diagnosed with common mental health disorders than women, the gap was closer when they were asked whether they had felt "very depressed"'.

Alan Savill's son Ian was twenty-three when he killed himself, and his story is one that not only epitomises all that is wrong with the way we treat those even with mental health problems, but also highlights what can happen when men can't cope with something as seemingly insignificant as losing a job.

Ian had been diagnosed with depression years before his death. He'd kept it hidden from all but those close to him, including his employer. Then, having been injured at work, during the process of allowing him back he had to disclose to his bosses that he was on antidepressant medication. From that moment onwards Alan told me everything changed.

'Ian was immediately ostracised by his colleagues. He was no longer allowed to get close to them in case he somehow affected their behaviour, and gradually he started getting fewer and fewer shifts.' Alan says Ian was soon asked to leave the company and the job he loved, all because he was taking tablets that kept him healthy.

Suddenly Ian was jobless, and Alan says he soon felt

worthless as a man. 'He clearly felt terrible being unable to provide for his family and without warning, three days before Christmas, decided he'd had enough.'

If he'd had a back injury and was taking pain killers to help him work, he would not have been treated in that disgusting way by his employer. Alan now works with the charity Survivors of Bereavement from Suicide, helping those affected by the loss of a loved one, and says the number of families grieving for a young man is staggering.

The reason we may require a bespoke mental health service is because the way men insist on hiding their problems means a different approach is required to find a solution. Simply telling these men 'you need to talk' is far too blunt and intimidating.

It's the very beginnings of those emotionally illiterate male minds that desperately need to be addressed. For the younger generations, we still have time to give them the opportunity to learn the skills required to process their emotions healthily.

The chief executive of the suicide prevention charity Papyrus, Ged Flynn, says that, despite having worked in the field of young suicide prevention for seven years, it's almost impossible to ever know the true reason behind why people decide to take their own lives.

Alongside the fact many men never fully divulge their innermost problems, Ged also told me that 'when you listen to all the stories you hear from families about someone suffering from X problem or Y problem, what you often realise is that they died because of X, Y and Z. It's always more complex than it looks.'

But he does accept that '75–80 per cent of suicides are male, so there must be something happening to men or about men that puts them more at risk'. When I suggested it may be the way we institutionalise masculinity, he says it's definitely a major factor.

A close friend of mine recently lost one of his school friends to suicide and, when I asked him what had happened, he could only say it was 'totally unexpected'. My friend told me his mate had always been happy, and they'd even been on holiday together just two weeks before he killed himself. Just days before his death, this guy had reached out to some of his mates, telling them he was having a tough time. Rather than jump to his aid, they all suggested they 'discuss it over the weekend' when they got together. Only he didn't make it to the weekend.

On reflection, my friend and his mates have accepted that, as a group, they'd all skirted around any conversations involving their emotional well-being for the entirety of their friendship. They have now vowed to be more honest with each other in the future, but, unfortunately, it's too little too late for their friend.

In the course of researching this book I must have spoken with six or seven people who knew young men who had committed suicide. Almost all of them said that it happened 'out of the blue'. Each time I heard that phrase, the more infuriated I became. It's not that I blame the individuals around those who died, but if we allowed ourselves to be more open and encouraged others to do likewise, I'd bet a lot of those young male lives could have been saved.

But mental health isn't just about suicide prevention. As I'm only too aware of, things can happen during a young man's life that masculinity doesn't allow him to properly deal with. Mark Mercer has been a bereavement counsellor for eighteen years and considers the fact that men don't cry in front of other men as one of the main reasons men's grief stays unresolved much longer than women's. He says 'most of our tears are shed when we are alone, perhaps while driving our vehicles. In all too many cases, our hot tears become a deep-freeze of anger or rage', while also warning that 'most very angry men are very sad men'.

In early 2017, Prince Harry spoke openly about the impact of losing his mother in 1997. He now admits to having locked away his emotions for nearly twenty years, spending his teens and early twenties determined not to think about her. 'I can safely say that losing my mum at the age of twelve, and therefore shutting down all of my emotions for the last twenty years, has had a quite serious effect on not only my personal life but my work as well.'

He says bottling up his grief meant he was often on the verge of violence, describing 'two years of chaos' as he grew up. He now admits it was only when he sought counselling and opened up about his feelings that he began to recover.

Opening up and being honest must have been far more difficult for Harry than it is for most. Not only is he constantly in the public eye – most especially on the day of Diana's funeral when, as a twelve-year-old, he walked behind her coffin on live television – the Royal Family is also expected to be the embodiment of the British 'stiff upper-lip'. In fact, despite the thousands of war memorials, funerals and sombre occasions the Queen has attended, the first time she cried in public was when her royal yacht *Britannia* was decommissioned. It's hardly surprising, therefore, that Harry's candid admission made headline news across the UK and beyond.

If, like me, you're not a fanatical monarchist, you may question the importance of someone like Harry speaking out. Well, working as I do at LBC Radio, I can tell you that the phone lines were swamped with people wanting to share their stories with us, even admitting it was the first time they'd ever spoken to anyone other than a doctor. What's more, the Chair of the Royal College of Psychiatrists, Sir Simon Wessley, said that Harry's admission had achieved more in terms of communicating mental health issues in a 25-minute interview than he'd managed to achieve in a 25-year career. That's not to say Simon hasn't done an excellent job, but we just can't underestimate the power of honesty. And while the rich and famous may get the headlines, every single one of us has the power to change the way society approaches mental health.

• • •

The talk of being 'tough' and 'strong' doesn't only prohibit some men admitting they have a mental health problem. There's both scientific and anecdotal evidence to suggest that our sense of masculinity prevents us seeking treatment for life-threatening illnesses.

Take cancer, as a perfect example. While the lifestyle choices many men make mean we're 15 per cent more likely to develop cancer, according to Cancer Research UK we're also 36 per cent more likely to die from it than women.

Why? Well, the *British Journal of Cancer* tells us 44 per cent of men with prostate cancer delayed visiting their GP about their symptoms for three months or more. In contrast, only 8 per cent of women with breast cancer symptoms put off getting help.

Yes, you read that right. We're more likely to die sooner because we steadfastly refuse to seek medical help until it's too late. The advent of the Sat Nav may have helped us to avoid the shame of having to ask for help with car journeys, but when it comes to our mental and physical wellbeing we're still as determined as ever to drive down those dead ends. Imagine being so trapped by your own masculinity that you're too tough to ask for medical help.

A team of researchers at Rutgers University set out to question this very issue and came up with a fairly predictable set of results. They say those men who hold the traditional beliefs that they should be tough, strong and emotionally restrained were far less likely to seek medical treatment than men who ignore the constraints of masculinity. What's more, the study also found that men are more likely to choose to see a male doctor, despite the fact they're likely to be more candid about their ailments to a female doctor.

Diana Sanchez was one of the psychologists leading the study and said 'that's because they don't want to show weakness or dependence to another man, including a male doctor'. She believes men are more likely to be honest about their illness with a female doctor because to be vulnerable with a woman risks no loss of status.

The life expectancy for men in the UK is currently three years less than that for women. Men's death rates are one of those things the MRAs shout about as 'proof' men are second class citizens, but we simply don't look after our minds or our bodies in the same way women do. Aside from the pressure to maintain the facade of strength, perhaps it's the way we're raised to take more risks and be less nurturing to ourselves that convinces us to live far unhealthier lifestyles.

Over the past few years, as with many of these issues, there's been a gradual realisation that something drastic has to happen to change the narrative around men and the way they view their own health. We're not invincible, no matter how much we'd like to convince ourselves otherwise, and there are now far more organisations than ever focused on helping men to overcome those barriers preventing them from seeking help.

One of those is the charity Movember which, since 2003, has been convincing men to get sponsored to grow a moustache throughout the month of November. In just fourteen years Movember has become the biggest non-governmental contributor to men's health around the world. It has raised upwards of £500 million and has donated to over 1,200 global projects involved with men's health. It recognised the gap between the life expectancy of men and women and aims to 'reduce the number of men dying prematurely by 25 per cent' by the end of the next decade.

I spoke to Justin Coghlan, one of the co-founders of Movember, about the importance of a male-led movement when it comes to promoting men's health. He said the main reason it started was because 'we looked around and we saw amazing things happening to help women and children, and there was almost nothing for men'.

Coghlan says he's learned that 'you can't simply tell men to do stuff', adding that 'if you try and dictate to them they usually act negatively against it'. He believes men's reluctance to take care of themselves can be attributed to the fact they 'think it's macho to constantly assume they're healthy'. With this in mind, Coghlan made sure that Movember's success has come through encouraging men to engage in discussions about their health without appearing too preachy. They not only encourage raising money through moustache-growing, they also encourage shoulder-to-shoulder conversations via sporting events, over a beer or through 'man-tripping'. Coghlan really wants men to have proper conversations with their friends. 'When you talk to guys in their early twenties they have a great group of mates … but, by their forties, something big will happen in their lives and their support network has often vanished by this stage.' Most important of all, he recognises that 'once you know you have someone to chat to, it's a game changer'.

It's a superb example of an organisation that recognises the different approaches required to engage men who've been taught to ignore their problems and offers bespoke activities to suit their needs.

• • •

While we're still a long way from revolutionising masculinity for good, for now Martin Seager has a sensible solution. He says we need to co-opt the 'tough, strong' traditionally masculine narrative, and teach men that speaking out and being honest is an indication of far greater strength and toughness.

You only need look at what happened to the man I met in the pub to understand the importance of speaking about your own grief. The trauma of Alan's incident coupled with witnessing his father fight back his tears led him down a path of suppression, misery and near-death that's lasted for more than fifty years.

The director of the Mental Health Foundation is Mark Rowland and he says that 'mental health is so central to our experience of being alive that if we're ever to rise to the challenge of preventing mental health problems, it will be because men feel more able to share when they are vulnerable'. He says 'it takes courage to be open and honest about mental health, but when suicide is the leading cause of death in young men, we all have a responsibility to push for cultural change'. Mark's solution is to try and change the discourse around the way we express ourselves, ensuring it's 'not about being more of a man, but being more in touch with our humanity'.

The true number of men struggling with their mental health is probably far higher than we'll ever know, but as each one of us drops our guard, whether we have a mental health problem or not, we make it easier for the next man to follow suit. For those still stuck in the past, we have to find avenues to allow them to express themselves. We can help release men from the pressure, both for ourselves and for the next generation.

The offer of a friendly chat over a pint is one of the ways men can attempt to get the ball rolling on those discussions a friend may be desperately in need of.

Slowly but surely those avenues for self-expression are developing for us all, but more needs to be done to create conversations where, as a group, we allow ourselves to truly open up about how we feel.

Celebrities as diverse as former England football captain Rio Ferdinand, rapper Professor Green and all-round British national treasure Stephen Fry are speaking up about their personal mental battles, and all recommending talking as the best therapy.

We need more men like Jonny, Sam and Alan Savill who are willing to be frank about their experiences and spread the message that vulnerability is not weak and admitt that having a problem is a sign of strength. It's only through starting these conversations that we'll update the masculine social construct that stops us being honest to and about ourselves.

That masculinity is forced on almost every single one of us, and while many of us might make it through our lives without ever showing signs of psychological pain, our unwillingness to even talk about trivial matters in an honest and open way will only to serve to ensure those that desperately need to talk remain shut away.

For the men who do seek treatment, those providing mental health care have to recognise the constraints masculinity enacts on all these men. We need to update our thinking about engaging the older generations, while ensuring we don't make the same mistakes again with the generations to come.

When you think that 4,500 men are killing themselves every year in the UK, something clearly needs to be done. It's imperative that these conversations start, and they need to start now.

CHAPTER TWELVE

NOW WHAT?

To all of you who have made it this far, the first thing I'd like to do is to thank you. As I said at the very beginning of this book, I could totally understand why you'd feel no desire to listen to someone like me when it comes to the finer points of psychological and sociological theories on the masculine construct and the effect it can have on society as a whole.

All I hope to have achieved is to at least offer you some semblance of an argument outlining why it's important we start to recognise there may be a problem with our pursuit of masculinity.

I'm by no means the first person ever to broach this subject. There's an increasingly vocal cohort of men willing to step outside the expected norms their sex has taught them to abide by, and that must be roundly celebrated. I'm merely adding my voice to the choir.

But what can't be underappreciated is the reality that women recognised the issues masculinity can cause long before men did; it's just that we mostly chose to ignore their appeals for us to let it all go. It's their sex who has suffered the majority of injustices meted out by men's unwillingness to release the grip on the reins of power, but as is always the case with inequality, those suffering are the protestors and it falls to them to be the agents for change.

What I hope to have achieved is to highlight how, actually, it's not just others who are suffering at the expense of masculinity – it's also us. In doing so, I hope to have galvanised more men to join the calls for a masculine revolution.

As a man, I'm fully aware of the impact another man's opinion can have on us and that's why I hope, as someone who's experienced and perpetrated the horrors rampant masculinity can bring to the world, you might trust my judgement on it.

Men are more likely to listen to men – it's just the way we are as a sex. Whether we're in boardrooms, in a doctors' surgery or at the pub talking about football, when it comes to our day-to-day conversations, men are still more likely to actively engage with other men. We're mostly friends with other men, mostly work with other men and a lot of us still wrongly value a male voice as more knowledgeable than a female one. That's why it's so important for men to engage in the gender debates with other men.

I'm under no illusion that the words of one man in a book of this nature will have the desired effect so many of us would like. Quite honestly, if my words spare just one man from the torment that is the unwavering belief that traditional masculinity is the only standard for men, then I will consider my work successful.

We're never going to rid the world of all its violence and misogyny, but we should all recognise that there are ways in which we can provide other options and reduce the rates at which men are committing these acts.

We have a long way to go before we no longer value our manliness over our health and the overall wellbeing of society, but we have to keep pushing the agenda for a new, modern, tolerant masculinity. Imagine if the women fighting for the vote 100 years ago had given up or the civil rights movement had faltered when they were pushed back time and time again. These were both epic fights that took years of sacrifice and endurance, and, while neither have yet been won in their entirety, the world has come a hell of a long way. We men already hold most of the power and influence. Society still ensures the words of men travel further and are received with more deference than those of women, particularly by other men. So this is a battle of men against men. Nobody else is standing in our way.

It's now up to us to somehow persuade vast swathes of blokes that many of our efforts to appear typically masculine are damaging and certain behaviour needs to change; and, while that's not going to be easy, it's of the utmost importance. In completely re-evaluating what it means to be a man, we will empower young men to be the change that is so desperately needed in the world. And that has to happen now.

I hope you'll agree that much of what I've just said is very much common sense. Far too many young men are still brought up with the notion that their masculinity is not only something to be proud of, but is also something that should be roundly protected from any 'feminisation' they may stumble across.

To the men reading this, which one of us can honestly say we haven't dreamt of having the perfect body, the big house, the fast car and the beautiful wife, all of which we can call our own. For many, these ideals are as much a part of being male as having a penis. We genuinely believe that we're naturally drawn to all those things, but it simply isn't true. We've been indoctrinated from the moment of birth, and we now need to understand that our own masculinity is an amalgamation of all the different influences we've experienced throughout our lives.

Grow up in a house where your father is violent, you're more likely to be violent. Grow up in an environment where women were treated with disrespect, you're more likely to disrespect women. If your parents followed the traditions of the stay-at-home mother and career-driven father, it's hardly surprising if you end up following suit.

But it goes way beyond parental influence, as we already know. Every generation may have had slightly different notions of masculinity, but the common threads are usually the same. We've raised young men this way for so long that it's only by slowly chipping away at each trope associated with masculinity that we will gradually release those pressures to conform to its rigidity.

There's already been a huge generational shift when it comes to how some younger men view their own masculinity. As the equality agenda has progressed, far fewer young men and women are brought up in the traditional and outdated ways our parents' generation were. Many of the young men I have spoken to recognise the privileges they experience by virtue of the fact that they are male, but very few of them were completely aware of the reality of many of the issues masculinity presents us with. While many men embrace the movement towards a more tolerant society, it's become snagged on a rising tide of fear and hatred. This means there's also been a rise in the number of men of all ages who feel traditional masculinity should somehow be protected, ensuring men don't lose their right to dominate their sphere of influence.

Not only is that ludicrously regressive, it's also unfeasible to think those of us who've evolved with each leap forward towards progression will not stand up against those who wish to undo much of the good work that's already been done. And that is why I hope you'll agree the issues I raise within this book are of the utmost importance not only for men but for society as a whole.

That's also why those of you who consider yourselves to be the 'good guys' aren't off the hook. It now falls on you to help redefine our masculinity, and banish once and for all the mentality of macho impunity that still exists among many groups of men. If you consider yourself to be a little more enlightened when it comes to your own sense of what it is to be a man, you have an obligation to add your voice to the growing number of men and women who wish to see an end to the traditional masculinity that creates so much chaos within our lives. It's only by increasing the regularity of our interventions that we can expect to see any real change.

I feel it's important to acknowledge that, at some points in this book, it may have appeared that I was being unduly harsh on men as a whole. And, while I accept that may have been true, it's because it's only through being brutally honest that we're able to understand how masculinity can morph into something toxic. In short, it's only by focusing on the negative outcomes that we're able to ensure mistakes aren't repeated and carried through the generations. Only then can we start to redevelop society to be more inclusive of all the varieties of men that exist in our wonderfully varied and diverse world.

What became increasingly obvious through my research is that there are some absolutely fantastic men who are already embodying all the changes so many of us would like to see. They're setting incredible examples for every generation to emulate, and each has their own unique reason for doing so. These men acknowledge their own experiences of masculinity and the role it played in bringing about negative behaviours, and have contributed to the vast jigsaw of reconstructing modern-day masculinity.

While I hope I have helped to identify the problems men in the 21st-century experience, it doesn't answer the obvious question that then follows: now what? If we know that change is required, what does that change look like?

From the moment young boys are born, we must allow them the freedom to explore every different avenue they might want to wander down. In doing so, they will naturally develop a greater sense of understanding of their place in this ever-changing world.

It's imperative that we stop pigeonholing boys through our language and the activities we enforce upon them, thus broadening their ability to empathise with those they come in to contact with.

We must teach young boys that understanding their emotions is the healthiest way they can interact with each other and understand themselves. That will allow them to grow and develop without repressing their feelings, and this means they will experience a greater sense of self as they deal with all the variety of experiences the world has to throw at them – be they positive or negative.

We have to understand that the decisions we make for our sons even in their earliest years can have a long-term effect on who they grow up to be. As fathers, we need to not only take a greater interest in the emotional welfare of our own sons, but also encourage more men to be involved in teaching, care roles and community support.

As our young boys grow up, they need to be taught how to better understand their sexuality. They must learn to value healthy relationships above visual stimuli, and seek the elation and heartache of real love rather than the corruptibility and blankness of porn.

These teenage boys need to experience care and compassion

to ensure they don't fall into the trap of spiralling anger and violence, and must be taught ways to manage their emotions that don't involve lashing out. This not only saves them from their own mental exasperation, but will also spare others the all-too-common suffering.

Our young men need to be taught that their actions not only have consequences for them, but can also have long lasting implications for those around them.

In order to prevent the cycle being continued, young men need to be encouraged to call out the undesirable behaviour they witness among their peer groups.

We must all drop the notion that our finances, physicality or promiscuity are the only ways in which we judge ourselves as success stories. We need to work together to create environments in which a more varied cache of men are accounted for and valued. We need to stop forcing men into a race for perfection. By acknowledging that imperfection isn't taboo and, actually, ought to be embraced, we will release the young men caught in the net of anxiety around their masculinity.

It's important we teach men and boys the values of a more equal society, not only to make way for those whose voices have been ignored, but also to remove the undue pressure on us to be in charge of everything in our lives. We must help young men understand the weight of the world doesn't have to be on their shoulders, and that women are willing and more than qualified to share the burden. They must also learn that the equality agenda is not about removing their rights, but about granting the freedom we've always enjoyed to others.

We need to look to the ways in which women have improved the lives of other women, and recognise that men have a great chance and ability to improve the lives of other men.

The conversations have begun, and young men are more comfortable opening up about their problems than they have ever been in the past, but, for the most part, we're still bound by the lessons we learned as children. That's not to say older generations are a write-off, but if we do want to make widespread societal change, we need to shift much of our focus onto the younger generations.

By reconstructing our understanding of what it means to be a man, we give ourselves the freedom to be the agents for change society so desperately needs.

I'm not saying this is a miracle cure, but it's hard to argue against the fact that alleviating men of the pressures enacted by so many aspects of masculinity will help create more rounded individuals and a fairer society.

Given how personal many of the topics I've discussed with you have been, I thought I'd share something I wrote on my blog back in 2014. I published this exactly a year to the day that my dad died, and it was only by reading it back I've realised why I've been so hard on myself and men in general.

I've come a long way from the twenty-year-old guy struggling to understand why he acted the way he did, and only wish I'd read a book like this before I turned into that person. But what's promising is that younger generations are growing up far more enlightened than mine. That's not to say they're off the hook, but many boys are shunning traditional masculinity in favour of a more relaxed and updated version. I have great faith that the next crop of young men will grow up in a world where macho pressures will continue to decrease.

But that goal will only be achieved if older generations allow younger men space to make these changes. That's why my one hope is that those of you who read this will do what you can to put this call to arms in place. Share these ideas with the men in your lives of all ages so we can all try to convince them that the pursuit of masculinity is out of touch with the modern world, and will only serve to make them out of touch, too.

CHAPTER THIRTEEN

AN APOLOGY FROM MY TWENTY-YEAR-OLD SELF

Dear Women (and some men),
    I'm sorry.

I'm sorry for all the things I say and for the things I don't have the courage to say. I'm sorry for my actions, and for my continued weakness in inaction.

To all the women I call a slut, whether to your face or behind your back, I'm sorry. I don't understand how damaging that concept is.

To the women whose appearances I rate out of ten, I'm sorry. I don't realise I'm objectifying you.

To the women I chant 'get your tits out' to, I'm sorry. I'm trying to fit in.

To the women whose naked pictures I've helped circulate, I'm sorry. I hadn't thought about your right to privacy.

255

To those I share platonic relationships with, I'm sorry for the things I say when you aren't around. They would, I'm sure, deeply offend you.

To the men I've convinced to get involved on the pretence it was 'only a laugh', I'm sorry to you, too. I've made you a part of the problem and therefore helped perpetuate it.

And to all of you, everywhere, I'm sorry I don't put my hand up and say 'stop'.

I am oblivious to the consequences of my behaviour and for that I am truly sorry.

While it is no excuse, I fear I'm a fairly typical twenty-year-old 'lad'. I've simply bought into a shameful culture because I don't have the guts to be different – and that is my greatest shame.

When I was younger, my mind-set was altogether different but, for my sins, I have been swayed by a collection of belligerent alpha males, determined to prove their masculinity. In our collective pursuit of this fruitless ideal, we have lost sight of the harm we are doing both to those around us and to ourselves. In our bid to show we are dominant, we have become blinded by our weak-mindedness.

While I know I am no ring-leader, and by no means the biggest perpetrator, I'm sorry that I join in. I'm sorry I laugh with them, high five them and validate them; I'm sorry I make the problem worse.

My attitude to many of you is, at times, despicable. Often I know I am doing wrong, only to ignore those inner-doubts in the face of a cheap laugh. Worst of all, I don't really mean it. I genuinely don't. It's just easier to continue the facade. I'm pathetic, really.

I know I can be a better person and hope, one day, to have the courage to cast off these shackles of machismo. But until then, please forgive me – I know not what I do. I need educating, and quickly.

Yours ashamedly,
Chris Hemmings (aged twenty)